Business School

Unit 2

Cost analysis for planning and decision making

Written by Pauline Gleadle

129.67

200.0

180.0

Module Team

Dr Mike Lucas, *B292 Chair & Author*

Professor Jane Frecknall-Hughes, *Professional Certificate in Accounting Chair & Author*

Elizabeth R Porter, *Regional Manager & Author*

Stuart Munro, *Author*

Dr Vira Krakhmal, *Author*

Dr Pauline Gleadle, *Author*

Jonathan Winship, *Author*

Dr Jane Hughes, *Contributor*

Sam Cooper, *Programme Coordinator*

Emir Forken, *Programme Manager*

Dr Lesley Messer, *Head of Curriculum Operations*

Funmi Mapelujo, *Qualifications Manager*

Kelly Dobbs, *Curriculum Assistant*

External Assessor

Professor Stuart Turley, Manchester Business School

Critical Readers

Richard Davies

Dr Jane Hughes

Developmental Testers

Dr Teodora Burnand

Sam Cooper

Diane Jamieson

Sue Winship

Nicole Wright

Production Team

Simon Ashby, Media Developer

Martin Brazier, Media Developer

Jo Breen, Media Developer

Anne Brown, Media Assistant

Vicky Eves, Media Developer

Lee Johnson, Media Project Manager

Diane Hopwood, Rights Assistant

Dr Kelvin Street, Library

The Module Team wishes to acknowledge use of some material from B680 *The Certificate in Accounting*.

This publication forms part of the Open University module B292 *Management accounting*. Details of this and other Open University modules can be obtained from the Student Registration and Enquiry Service, The Open University, PO Box 197, Milton Keynes MK7 6BJ, United Kingdom (tel. +44 (0)845 300 60 90; email general-enquiries@open.ac.uk).

Alternatively, you may visit the Open University website at www.open.ac.uk where you can learn more about the wide range of modules offered at all levels by The Open University.

To purchase a selection of Open University materials visit www.ouw.co.uk, or contact Open University Worldwide, Walton Hall, Milton Keynes MK7 6AA, United Kingdom for a brochure (tel. +44 (0)1908 858793; fax +44 (0)1908 858787; email ouw-customer-services@open.ac.uk).

The Open University

Walton Hall

Milton Keynes

MK7 6AA

First published 2011. Second edition 2012.

© 2012 The Open University

Edited and designed by The Open University.

Typeset in India by OKS Prepress Services, Chennai.

Printed in the United Kingdom by Cambrian Printers, Aberystwyth.

ISBN 978 1780 0 7381 1

2.1

FSC

Mixed Sources

Product group from well-managed forests and other controlled sources

Cert no. TT-COC-2200
www.fsc.org
© 1996 Forest Stewardship Council

Contents

Introduction

Unit 2 builds upon Unit 1 which acted as an overall introduction to the module in terms of what managers do and the organisations in which they work. In Unit 1, you learned about the nature and objectives of organisations, the nature of management and the role of management accounting in the management process, the role of information and information systems in organisations and the opportunities offered by IT in managing organisations. Unit 2 turns to the topic of cost analysis for the important management functions of planning and decision making. There are five sessions in this unit, corresponding with each of the unit's main aims.

Session 1 looks at different types of costs: the nature and behaviour of fixed, variable, stepped fixed and semi-variable costs. An understanding of basic cost behaviour is essential to the work of management accountants.

Session 2 discusses the role of costs in decision making. This will help explain why organisations need to know the costs of products, processes and services and so why they need costing systems. By the end of this session, you will be able to discuss the nature of production costs in terms of materials, labour and overheads and you will also be able to explain the nature of different non-production costs.

Session 3 considers some applications of the cost concepts, specifically, the use of marginal costs, cost-volume-profit analysis and contribution analysis in costing and decisions. While you will learn to use these tools in different ways, you will also learn about the limitations of cost-volume-profit analysis, as well as how to calculate the profit maximising production plan where there is limited demand and one limiting factor (i.e., a scarce resource such as labour or raw materials).

Session 4 looks at absorption costing as an alternative to marginal costing. You will learn about the allocation, apportionment and absorption of overhead costs under absorption costing and you will learn about the alternative approach of marginal costing and the effects of the two costing approaches on inventory valuation and reported profits. In Session 4 you will also learn about the use of cost information in pricing decisions, including the calculation of 'full cost' based prices in order to generate a specified return on investment.

Finally, in **Session 5** you will look at two key concepts within management accounting: relevant costs for decision making and a specific type of relevant cost called 'opportunity cost'. You will learn how to calculate the relevant costs for materials, labour and overheads as well as how to calculate the relevant costs associated with non-current assets.

By the end of Unit 2, you should have a clear idea about the nature of cost analysis for planning and decision making and be able to apply and explain the techniques covered.

Learning aims and outcomes of Unit 2

Upon completion of Unit 2 you are expected to understand and be able to explain:

1   the different types of costs
2   the role of costs in decision making
3   the use of marginal costs, cost-volume-profit analysis and contribution analysis in costing and pricing decisions
4   absorption costing as an alternative to marginal costing
5   relevant costs for decision making.

SESSION 1 **The different types of costs**

Introduction

Upon completion of Session 1 you are expected to be able to:

- describe the nature and behaviour of fixed, variable, stepped fixed and semi-variable costs
- use the high-low method to separate costs into their fixed and variable elements
- use the line of best fit method to ascertain (approximately) the magnitude of fixed and variable costs
- draw graphs showing the behaviour of different types of cost
- explain why costs need to be classified as direct/indirect, full, marginal, etc., to be meaningful for planning and decision making.

During this session, we shall look at the differences between four common categories of cost – direct, indirect, variable and fixed.

1.1 How costs are classified

Costs can be classified in several ways, the principal classifications being:

- variable and fixed
- direct and indirect.

The classification into variable and fixed costs is used in **marginal costing** (a costing approach in which variable costs are charged to product units and fixed costs are charged against profit as a period expense, that is, not charged to specific units of output or activity). The classification into direct and indirect costs is used in **absorption costing** (a costing approach that charges both direct costs and indirect costs, and crucially, fixed and variable costs, to units of output or activity). These approaches to costing are described in Sessions 3 and 4 of this unit.

There are other ways of classifying costs, such as distinguishing between **actual** and **standard cost** or **controllable** and **non-controllable** cost. These classifications are relevant in standard costing and budgetary control and they are dealt with in Unit 4 of this module.

1.2 Variable and fixed costs

The relevant range is the range of activity for which our assumptions about constant fixed and constant unit variable costs hold true. These assumptions are discussed later in Session 3.

The distinction between variable and fixed costs is the basis of marginal costing. Once we know what the variable and fixed costs are, we can work out the cost of a unit of output at any level of activity, within the so-called **relevant range**. When we cannot accurately predict the future level of activity (which happens often), this classification of costs gives us a powerful management tool for evaluating results under different levels of activity.

Variable costs

Variable costs are a function of the level of activity. For example, if activity doubles, the variable cost also doubles; if activity trebles, the variable cost trebles. In the case of a car factory, variable costs include the material content of each vehicle (e.g., the engine, body shell, glass, tyres, and so on).

Variable costs are sometimes referred to as the **marginal cost**.

To be more precise, marginal cost is the part of the cost of one unit of product or service which would be avoided if that unit were not produced, or which would increase if one extra unit were produced.

Fixed costs

Fixed costs are any other costs that are not variable. Fixed costs are, in essence, a function of time, not activity level or volume of output. They are the costs that would be incurred even if activity is zero. In a car factory, fixed costs include the rent, depreciation of equipment, management salaries and so on. Now let us consider these ideas in an activity.

Activity 1.1 ....

In an accounting practice, which of the following costs are variable and which are fixed?

(a) an annual software licence fee for use of accounting software throughout the practice

(b) advertising

(c) telephone

(d) secretaries' salaries

(e) wages paid to the office cleaners.

We have to examine these costs in the context of the facts to establish their classification.

Allow ten minutes for this activity.

Feedback ....

(a) A software licence of this type will be a fixed cost. It will only change if the level of activity shifts outside the relevant range. For example, if the licence fee covers five computers, it would only change if the practice grew and needed more.

(b) Advertising is usually regarded as fixed, but you must consider the circumstances. This is because advertising expenditure usually arises 'up front' as a result of a management decision, rather than being determined in a 'cause and effect' manner by units produced or sold.

(c) Most telephone bills can be divided into a fixed rental component and a variable usage element. The rental is clearly fixed and, if the usage is related to activity in an accounting practice, the usage is variable. Where calls cannot be traced to individual clients, they are normally treated as costs of the period, that is, they would be treated in the same way as fixed costs are treated.

(d) Secretaries' salaries will be a fixed cost.

(e) The wages paid for office cleaning are normally treated as fixed unless there is a direct link between activity in the accounting practice and cleaning the office.

Contribution

An important concept in connection with variable costs is **contribution**. It is the difference between the variable cost of sales and the sales revenue generated and is an abbreviation of the phrase 'contribution towards fixed costs'. It can be calculated at the unit cost level or in aggregate for all production. The concept of contribution is very important in marginal costing and it is considered in detail in Session 3 of this unit.

1.3 Cost behaviour

Figures 1 to 4 are graphs showing the pattern of costs in relation to the volume of activity, based on the following information for a period. The level of activity can be expressed in terms of the units of production or the level of service activity (Figure 1).

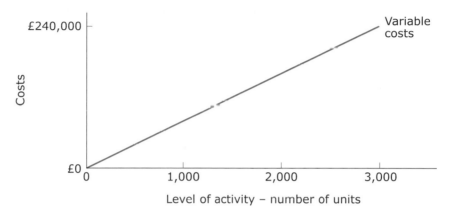

Figure 1 Variable costs

Variable costs per unit	£80
Maximum output in the period	3,000 units
Variable costs (at maximum output)	£240,000
Fixed costs	£100,000

We can calculate variable cost (VC) per unit as follows:
Max. output in period=3,000 units
VC at max. output= £240,000
VC per unit=£240,000/ 3,000=£80 (assuming fixed costs remain constant at £100,000).

The relevant range for which these relationships hold is 0 – 5,000 units.

Note how the variable costs are proportional to the level of activity and how they are always zero when the level of activity is zero.

Note also how the fixed costs remain constant at all levels of activity within the relevant range (Figure 2).

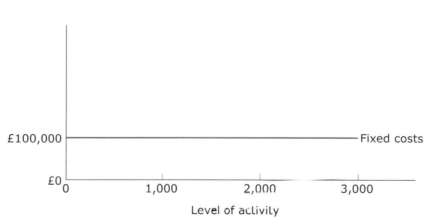

Figure 2 Fixed costs

The two graphs can be combined to show total costs (Figure 3).

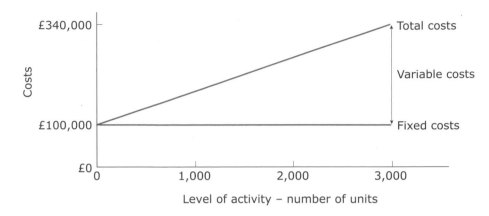

Figure 3   Total costs

At a production level of 3,000 units, the total cost is £340,000, resulting in a unit cost of £113.33. Had the production level been 1,800 units, the total cost would be £244,000 (fixed costs of £100,000 plus variable costs of £144,000) and the resulting unit cost is £135.56. As the volume of activity declines, the unit cost increases. Conversely, as the volume of activity increases, the unit cost decreases.

Activity 1.2

Why does the unit cost change?

Spend about five minutes to produce your answer.

Feedback   ....

The reason is that, with reducing volumes, each unit has to bear proportionately more of the fixed costs and, with increasing output, proportionately less of the fixed costs.

The changing unit cost of production is shown in Figure 4. To calculate the unit cost, divide the total of fixed and variable costs by the number of units produced. An example is given in Activity 1.3.

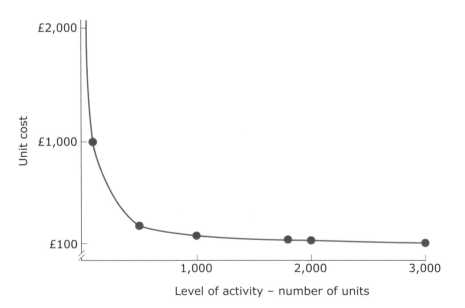

Figure 4   The changing cost per unit as the level of activity changes

Activity 1.3   ....

Using the following information for a period, calculate the unit cost at production levels of 2,000, 4,000 and 5,000 units of output.

Fixed costs	£264,000
Variable costs per unit	£279

Spend no more than 15 minutes on this activity.

Feedback   ....

Production levels	2,000 units £	4,000 units £	5,000 units £
Variable cost per unit	279	279	279
Total variable costs	558,000	1,116,000	1,395,000
Fixed costs	264,000	264,000	264,000
Total costs	822,000	1,380,000	1,659,000
Divide total costs by no. units	2,000	4,000	5,000
Unit cost	= 411	= 345	= 331.80

It is important to bear in mind that both fixed and variable costs may only behave in this way over a relevant range. For example, within the relevant range (see Figure 5), unit variable costs are assumed to be constant. Beyond this range, they are not. (This could be due to bulk discounts in purchasing materials, for example.) In the following example, variable costs (per unit) are only constant between 600 and 1,200 units.

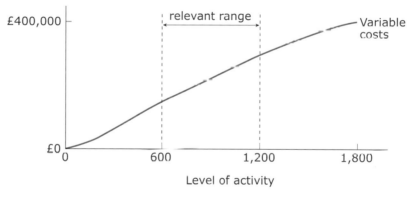

Figure 5   The relevant range

1.4 Stepped fixed costs

Fixed costs are often only fixed within a range of activity levels. Frequently, when we refer to fixed costs, they are assumed to be fixed whatever the level of activity, but fixed costs do change. The term used to describe the concept of change in fixed costs is 'stepped costs'. These can be described as being constant within a specified range of output but changing when outside this range. This is illustrated in Figure 6. Above 2,000 units, a new level of fixed costs is reached.

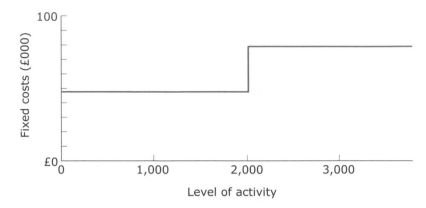

Figure 6   Stepped fixed costs

The concept can again be illustrated by an accounting practice. For a given level of clients, the practice can cope with the current number of accountants but, at a certain level of activity, the pressures of work will mean an additional accountant needs to be employed. If on a full time contract, this extra accountant would be a stepped cost, that is, an increased fixed cost. (If an accountant could be employed on a casual, part time basis, this would resemble more closely a variable cost.)

1.4.1   Determining fixed versus variable costs

The material, labour and machine resources needed to make a unit of a particular product (or provide a unit of a particular service), could be measured and then divided over the units to be produced, to give a unit variable cost. However, in practice things are not always as simple as that as many costs are semi-variable, with both variable and fixed components. Despite this complication, many planning and decision making activities require an understanding of how costs change as the level of output changes. This requires separating costs into their fixed and variable elements.

There is a number of techniques, of varying degrees of sophistication, available to management for estimating fixed and variable costs, but you should always bear in mind that greater and greater levels of accuracy are usually more and more expensive to attain. Such levels of accuracy may also take longer to achieve because of the amount of information that has to be processed.

Organisations must always keep in mind that information has a cost and that it is pointless to have more detail and accuracy than necessary. The following sections describe two techniques that could be applied for the purpose of estimating fixed and variable costs.

The high-low method

The high-low or range method is a technique for splitting mixed costs into their fixed and variable elements. It is simple and quick but will often not be very accurate. Suppose a business had recorded the following costs for electricity relative to units of production from the factory.

	Electricity cost (£)	Units made
January	10,000	11,000
February	15,000	20,000
March	12,000	13,000
April	9,000	10,000
May	10,000	11,000
June	11,000	12,000
July	14,000	18,000
August	13,000	17,000
September	12,000	13,000
October	11,000	11,000
November	11,000	12,000
December	12,000	14,000

First, identify the periods with the highest and lowest production – here, the months of February and April.

	Units	£
High	20,000	15,000
Low	10,000	9,000

You can see that these costs are not purely variable otherwise they would double as the output doubles.

You can now assume that the increase in costs must arise from the variable part of the costs. So, the extra 10,000 units cause the additional costs of £6,000. This implies variable costs of £0.60 per unit.

If the variable costs are £0.60 per unit, 10,000 units would cause £6,000 total variable costs. At this output, the total costs are £9,000 so the fixed costs must amount to £3,000.

You can check the fixed costs by looking at the output levels chosen. At 20,000 units, variable costs would be £12,000. As total costs are £15,000, fixed costs must be £3,000 as before.

Assessing costs using a scatter graph

When plotting a line of best fit, you can use a ruler and move this along until the line you have drawn best fits the data, so minimising the distance between the data points and the line. This line is then the line of best fit.

Scatter graphs plot data points on a graph and are useful as another means of examining the relationship between fixed and variable costs. By drawing in the line of best fit, which plots a line which best fits the spread of the data, we are, in effect, setting out the total cost line (see Figure 7). This meets the vertical axis at an activity level of zero, so the total costs at that point must be the fixed costs. It follows that if we take the total costs at a particular level of activity, deduct the fixed costs and divide the resulting answer by the level of activity, we arrive at the variable cost per unit.

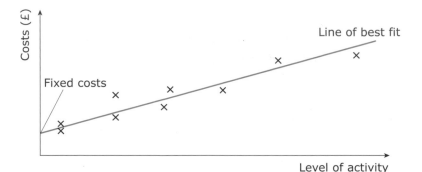

Figure 7   Using a scatter graph to find the line of best fit

A scatter graph is a useful visual insight into the relationship between fixed and variable costs and, indeed, can be regarded as superior to the high-low method which uses only two data points. However, remember that it is only a guide to the relationship: ultimately, the precise answer can only be calculated by a detailed analysis of the cost data. Such detailed analysis can be carried out using regression and correlation analysis which are discussed in Unit 5.

Now that we have explored cost behaviour in terms of fixed and variable costs, we introduce the notion of direct versus indirect costs.

1.5 Direct and indirect costs

This distinction is important and forms the basis of absorption costing which we will cover in Session 4 of this unit. The following definitions are attributed to Horngren et al. (1999).

Direct costs

Direct costs are all costs that can be directly attributed to a **cost object** and that can be traced to it in an economically feasible (cost effective) way. A cost object is defined as anything for which a separate measurement of costs is desired.

Indirect costs

Indirect costs are all costs that cannot be *directly* traced to a cost object in an economically feasible way. Indirect costs are allocated to the cost object using a cost allocation method.

Horngren et al. (1999, p. 32) give the example of a tennis racket as a cost object. The cost of the carbon fibre used to make the racket is a direct cost because it can be easily traced to the racket. However, the cost of lighting in the factory where the racket is made will be an indirect cost. This is because, although lighting helped in the manufacture of the racket (the workers needed to see), it is not cost effective to try to determine exactly how much lighting cost was used for a specific racket.

Whether a cost is direct or indirect depends on the cost object.

Indirect costs are also known as **overheads**.

Activity 1.4 ....

The following list shows typical costs for a customised sports car manufacturer. Decide whether the following costs are direct or indirect:

(a) component parts

(b) production labour

(c) depreciation of manufacturing equipment.

Spend about five minutes on this activity.

Feedback ....

(a) Component parts are clearly a direct cost of production and are variable – double the output and you double the number of components used. Each component can be directly identified with a unit of output.

(b) Similarly, production labour can be directly traced to particular products. However, it is important to recognise that, while the component parts are directly related to output and their costs are, in fact, variable, this is not necessarily the case with production labour. If the production line stops, the production operatives' wages still have to be paid. However, this in no way changes the nature of these wages. They are a direct cost incurred making a particular product.

(c) Depreciation of manufacturing equipment is an indirect production cost. Manufacturing equipment also depreciates, for example, through the passing of time or through obsolescence, as new, better equipment will come on to the market.

As you can see from these examples, it is necessary to remember that we are considering whether costs are direct or indirect relative to a particular product. Hence, component parts and production labour are directly linked to the particular product in contrast to depreciation which is not so related

We shall consider the way in which indirect costs are allocated to cost objects, in particular circumstances, in greater detail later in this unit.

Summary

In this session, you have learned about the importance of understanding cost behaviour in terms of fixed versus variable cost elements. You have also learned about the necessity of classifying costs as either direct or indirect. Finally, perhaps the overriding message of this unit concerns the need for people to be able to describe costs as fixed or variable and so on if they are to be able to understand cost behaviour in relation to goods or services provided. The next session builds upon the concepts covered in Session 1 in order to help you understand more about costs and decision making.

SESSION 2 Costs and decision making

Introduction

Upon completion of Session 2 you are expected to be able to:

- explain why organisations need to know the costs of products, processes and services
- distinguish between cost objects, cost units and cost centres
- explain why organisations need costing systems
- discuss the nature of production costs in terms of materials, labour and overheads
- explain the nature of different non-production costs.

2.1 Why organisations need to know the costs of products, processes and services

Ascertaining the cost of something is an essential part of effective management in an organisation. This applies to the commercial, not-for-profit and public sectors of the economy. In fact, it applies to all organisations, whatever their nature and form. An organisation without the necessary understanding of its cost structure and cost control is rather like a rudderless ship, lacking clear direction and at risk of breaking up when it meets the shore.

Costs are shown in external financial statements (such as the income statement) but what is disclosed about them is determined by the needs of reporting to shareholders or other stakeholders. Such information may provide a useful insight into overall performance but it is insufficiently detailed to be an in-depth analysis of specific activities, such as the labour cost of an individual product or how much a particular service costs. In this context, costing comes into its own. It provides a powerful management tool to monitor and plan activities. In any organisation, it is necessary to define clearly the nature of the product or services provided. This, in turn, will be the basis for defining the cost structure. The **cost unit** is defined as the unit of product or service for which cost is computed. Hence, a cost unit for a fruit juice factory might be a carton of fruit juice while the cost unit for a firm of professional accountants could take the form of a given year's tax computation for a particular client (depending on the type of work undertaken). Normally, the management of an organisation in the commercial and not-for-profit sectors, or the funding agencies in the public sector, decide what is a convenient cost unit.

Costs for decision making use the same source data as costs shown in financial statements, but they are often calculated differently.

2.2 Different cost classifications

We can identify a number of different classifications for cost, as follows.

- **By nature** – this would include material, labour or expenses. Classifying costs by nature can also be termed **subjective** classification.

- **By purpose** – direct or indirect. We introduced the distinction in Session 1 and will explore it further in this session. Classifying costs by purpose can also be termed **objective** classification.

- **By function** – for example, production, administration or selling.

- **By behaviour** – fixed, variable, semi-variable, stepped fixed. These concepts were introduced in Session 1 and will be further explored in this session.

- **Normal/abnormal** – this considers whether unusual events have influenced costs.

- **Controllable/non-controllable** – this is concerned with whether the manager, within whose area of the organisation a cost is incurred, can influence the cost.

- **Relevant/non-relevant** – this distinction is used in decision making and is covered in Session 5 of this unit.

Cost centre is the term used to describe where in an organisation costs are gathered and then attributed to the units of output. Normally, cost centres consist of departments. By way of contrast, the term cost object refers to any thing or activity for which a separate measurement of costs is desired. An example of a cost object would be the cost of rendering a service to a hospital patient. Other examples would include the cost of a product, the cost of a process or a department.

2.3 Why organisations need costing systems

Now that you appreciate how many different classifications are possible for costs, you can begin to understand why organisations need costing systems.

As certain activities will have the same types of costs irrespective of the individual organisation, entities in the same trade or sector may have very similar cost structures. In the public sector, for example, hospital trusts will all have similar costs and this drives the way in which they collect and report cost information. In higher education, the government-financed funding councils specify how costs are to be reported.

The need to comply with external reporting requirements focuses organisations on determining the costs that have to be identified to meet those requirements. This is also the case for commercial and not-for-profit organisations. The way they calculate their costs is governed, to some extent at least, by the external reporting requirements of their sector and the regulators concerned.

The accurate measurement of cost, however, is also important for several reasons, including:

- providing a basis for assessing past performance

- planning for future operations

- monitoring actual performance against budget

- assisting in decision making

- assisting in cost reduction and control.

Let us consider these factors in more detail by looking at the case of a window manufacturer supplying standard products to the house-building industry.[1]

Activity 2.1 ....

What cost information does the window manufacturer's management require?

Reflect on this activity for five minutes.

Feedback ....

The basic requirements of an accounting system are to identify, organise, classify, record, summarise and communicate information. As part of these functions, the accounting system has to measure the result of the organisation's operations in financial terms. The usual aim of the window manufacturer's business is to make a profit. Therefore, managers need to know whether the business has been operating profitably during the last year and, more importantly, whether it is currently profitable. Management is also about planning. An important source of information that management uses for this is data about costs incurred. While this information would be captured by the financial reporting system, managers need more detailed management accounting information, such as profitability of individual products, budget variances and so on.

Activity 2.2 ....

How does the window manufacturer assess past operations and future plans?

Take five minutes for this activity.

Feedback ....

The window manufacturer would probably assess both past operations and future plans by calculating gross profit and net profit, two terms we consider next.

Gross profit, sometimes called **gross margin**, is calculated by subtracting the **cost of goods sold** from sales. **Indirect expenses** must subsequently be subtracted before arriving at a **net profit**.

The key is to establish whether total revenue from the sale of windows exceeds the total costs incurred in their provision for sale. If they were manufactured (as opposed to bought in ready for resale), the gross profit would be calculated as follows (figures and dates are assumed for the sake of this example).

Gross profit calculation for the year ending 31 December 2010

	£
Sales	2,000,000
Less: Cost of goods sold	(1,800,000)
Gross profit	200,000

This calculation uses the sales and the cost of goods sold, which includes labour and material costs incurred as well as production indirect costs to arrive at the gross profit (or loss). However, as a basis for the day to day management of the factory, it provides us with only a limited insight into the company's performance.

[1] In the examples that follow, we focus on a window manufacturer and on one product only. You should note that if a firm were to produce one standard product only, problems of relating production costs to activities do not arise as all costs relate to that product. However, we are focusing on one product only for simplicity's sake in illustrating various key concepts for teaching purposes.

Activity 2.3

What is it about this information that restricts us to a limited view of the company's performance?

Take five minutes for this activity.

Feedback

If you want to use this information you need more details. This information is summarised. Decision makers need either disaggregated information or information that is organised and rendered useful. The information needs to be viewed in context if it is to be useful. For example, one essential piece of information, if it is to be useful, is a sense of scale – for example, how many windows were sold? Let us assume that 20,000 windows were sold. From this information, we can start to analyse the company's performance in a more meaningful way. Assuming that exactly 20,000 windows were produced during the year, we can now create a far more informative report than before.

Gross profit calculation for the year ending 31 December 2010

	£	Per window £
Sales	2,000,000	100
Less: Cost of production	(1,800,000)	(90)
Gross Profit	200,000	10

This report gives us a starting point for measuring the factory's detailed financial performance. Let us assume that all the windows were of the same specification and that inflation has not distorted the figures. From this information we have easily established that the average selling price was £100 and that each window cost an average of £90 to produce.

As a result, management can see that every unit made an average gross margin or gross profit of £10. This information can then be used for planning purposes. Is that enough per window? Is it enough gross profit overall – to cover expenses and result in an overall net profit? Can the gross profit be increased – either per window or overall?

These are the sorts of issues that management can only begin to consider when it has the necessary information. In the simple case of the window manufacturer, only when information about sales revenue, costs (including costs of production) and, therefore, gross and net profit per window, is available, does it become possible for management to consider revising its pricing, production levels and cost plans. Such individual unit cost information is vital for internal decision making (e.g., pricing) in the normal multi-product firm or in a services firm where different types of service offering are provided. This is discussed further in Unit 3.

We now begin to see the need for a costing system. Such a system relates production costs to activities – in this example, window production – and, in a commercial context, it enables us to establish the profitability of the activities. In the public sector or in a not-for-profit organisation, it provides the means of assessing the cost of providing a service or supplying a product.

Once management knows the level of activity, it can take a much more informed view of its operations. In the real world, accountants and managers would need to learn much more about the nature of the total cost of production of £1,800,000 for the window producer. For example, they would want to know how much the wood for the frames costs, how much the fittings cost, the cost of finishing and the charge for assembly labour, as well as the factory's expenses.

This simple example considered cost in a manufacturing context. If the organisation provided a service, similar information in terms of the cost of service delivery would be required. The precise nature of the cost information would depend on the purpose for which the cost information was to be used.

This unit will go on to consider the ways in which we both classify costs and summarise them to provide meaningful insights into the effective and ineffective management of an organisation.

2.4 The nature of production costs in terms of materials, labour and overheads

Cost cards are used to record all the elements of cost in a unit produced.

Production costs can be classified into three broad categories: materials, labour and overheads. These costs will be captured on a **cost card.** The cost card is a summary of costs that together make the total cost of one unit of a product, for example, a television or a meal. The term cost card is from an age that pre-dates computers, when costs were summarised on cards as they were incurred in the production process. Today, cost cards are usually computer print-outs, but the principle remains the same and the same information is recorded.

The information recorded will be the basic elements of cost – the materials used, the cost of labour and the proportion of indirect costs attributable to a particular unit of output.

The source of this information is described in the next few pages. See the example below of a cost card for a door (figures are assumed for the sake of the example).

An example of a cost card for a door

	Quantity	Unit cost	Total £
Material	20 kg	£4/kg	80
Labour	4 hours	£6/hour	24
Production overhead:			
Machining	4 hours	£2/hour	8
			112

You certainly need to understand the basic way in which cost data are captured. This is covered in more detail in Unit 3. The broad categories of cost in an organisation can generally be grouped under three main headings:

- material costs
- labour costs
- overheads or expenses.

Overheads relate to expenditure on labour, materials or services which cannot be economically identified with a specific saleable cost unit.

The broad categories of cost can be further classified as direct or indirect costs, a distinction we introduced in Section 1.5 of this unit.

A direct cost is one that can be specifically traced to a cost object. In a marketing context, for example, this object may be any one of several possible things other than just the product itself. Thus, in an analysis of sales territories, the salaries, commissions and expenses of sales personnel working exclusively in one territory constitute direct costs of that territory.

An indirect cost is one that cannot be traced to a specific cost object on anything other than a largely arbitrary basis. The narrower a cost object is (e.g., a customer or a product line), the greater will be the proportion of costs that are indirect, whereas the more broadly based a cost object is (e.g., a sales territory), the greater will be the proportion of costs that can be traced directly to it. It should be noted, however, that direct costs can be fixed or variable in nature (as can indirect costs), so directness should not be linked in any general way with variable costs alone, whether in a marketing setting or in any other instance.

Activity 2.4 ....

Nancy runs a design and assembly workshop for jewellery. She employs various craftspeople in her workshop. Classify the following costs as either direct or indirect (assume that the individual item of jewellery is the cost object):

(a) silver used in making necklaces, earrings and bracelets

(b) labour costs to shape and smelt jewellery

(c) salary of workshop supervisor

(d) cost of electricity for smelting.

Spend ten minutes on this activity.

Feedback ....

The direct costs would be (a) and (b) as they can be traced to specific items of jewellery. The indirect costs are likely to be (c) and (d) because they cannot be traced to specific items of jewellery.

'Could you be a little more precise than "umpteen million"?'

Direct/indirect and fixed/variable costs

You will remember that we discussed fixed and variable costs in Section 1.2 of this unit and that this distinction was crucial to understanding cost behaviour. You should note that costs may be simultaneously:

- direct and variable
- direct and fixed
- indirect and variable
- indirect and fixed.

An extended example of cost classification is given in Table 1.

Table 1   Examples of simultaneous direct/indirect and variable/fixed cost classifications

		Assignment of costs to cost object	
		Direct cost	**Indirect cost**
Cost behaviour pattern	**Variable cost**	*Cost object*: Assembled car	*Cost object*: Assembled car
		Example: Tyres used in assembly of car	*Example*: Power costs where power usage is metered only to the plant
		Cost object: Marketing department	*Cost object*: Marketing department
	Fixed cost	*Example*: Annual leasing cost of cars used by sales force representatives	*Example*: Monthly charge by corporate computer centre for marketing's share of corporate computer costs

(Source: Horngren et al., 1999, p. 38)

In Table 1, you can see that the tyres used in the assembly of a car are both variable and direct costs. Another example of a direct cost is the annual leasing cost of cars used by sales representatives, although you should note that these particular costs are fixed as they do not vary with the level of activity in terms of the number of cars assembled.

In terms of indirect costs, you can see from Table 1 that power costs, where usage is metered at the plant level only, constitute indirect but variable costs. Finally, the monthly charge by the corporate computer centre for marketing's share of corporate IT costs will be classified as simultaneously indirect and fixed because, again, these will not vary with the level of activity in terms of cars produced.

For a meaningful system of **cost control** to work, there must be a proper administrative system operating that enables costs to be monitored and allocated in order to calculate the cost of the product or service in an appropriate way.

The cost of each unit in a commercial organisation is then related to the sales revenue generated by selling each unit. In other words, once the cost of each unit is known, you can calculate the profit per unit sold.

Alternatively, you can set the selling price at a level that will generate the profit per unit that you wish to achieve.

Materials

There must be a proper system of inventory control for any meaningful costing system to operate. Such a system will need to control adequately the buying, receipt, storage and subsequent allocation of all items relevant to the cost of the product or service.

Labour costs

Labour costs have to be collected and charged to the appropriate goods or services. It is beyond the scope of this module to consider a detailed remuneration accounting system. You just need to be aware of the basic cost implications and how cost is charged to each unit of output.

In general, remuneration can be paid by two methods or combinations of them:

- time-related
- performance-related.

In a time-based system, an effective means of recording the time spent on a job is needed, which involves using time records. The remuneration is calculated by multiplying the time incurred on particular work by the appropriate rate per hour, minute, and so on.

These time records can be time sheets or, more likely, time-recording equipment.

In the case of performance-related pay (PRP), where the amount of pay depends on the efficiency or effectiveness of staff, systems have to be devised that record the level of relevant activity (e.g., the number of units produced). This is then used to pay employees at the appropriate rate. It is unusual for employees to be paid purely on a performance basis. Generally, they receive a minimum basic wage or salary and then their PRP is added to it.

The wages costs have to be allocated to products (cost units) or relevant cost centres. How this is done depends on the nature of the activities. For example, for individual discrete jobs (e.g., shipbuilding), it is based on the time spent on the job. In continuous processing of production (e.g., jam making), the labour costs incurred at each stage of the process are added together to arrive at the total labour cost, which this is then divided by the number of units of output produced, to obtain the labour cost per unit.

It is important to recognise that when charging labour to production, the associated labour costs, such as employer's pension contributions and other directly related costs, should also be charged to production.

Labour costs can be categorised as direct (relating to a specific item, e.g., table leg cutter wages) or indirect (relating to activities in general, e.g., factory supervisor salaries, rather than to specific individual items). Alternatively, they can be classified in terms of whether they are variable or fixed costs.

These classifications are not always straightforward. For example, when premium time, such as overtime, is involved, this is generally treated as an overhead cost. However, where a customer demands a job urgently, the cost of the overtime premium may well be charged directly to the job (as a direct cost). Similarly, the use of PRP has potential implications for the classification of costs between fixed costs (which remain unchanged for a given range of output within a defined period of time) and variable costs (which change as the level of activity varies). One way of avoiding these difficulties is to employ labour on a sub-contract basis.

Overhead costs: production and non-production

Production overhead costs include such items as supervisors' salaries and factory rent.

In addition to materials and labour costs, a wide range of other overhead costs needs to be recorded and collected so that an appropriate estimate of cost can be made. Many of these overhead costs will be periodic expenditure on items with which you will be familiar, including:

Business rates are a local property tax in the UK, and are treated as an overhead cost.

- rent and business rates (either related to production or non-production)

- insurance (either related to production or non-production)

- administration expenses (likely to be non-production)

- motor and travelling expenses (likely to be non-production).

These expenses are recorded in the accounting system and allocated or apportioned to the appropriate departments and analysed to aid decision making. In addition to these costs, which are paid in the normal course of trading, there are other costs, notably depreciation, which do not necessarily involve a cash outlay during the period under review. Depreciation (which is, of course, an operating cost), will have to be calculated using a suitable method.

Summary

In this session, we have explored why organisations need to know about costs and why they need costing systems. You have learned about different possible classifications for costs and the nature of production and non-production costs. In the next session, we shall consider some management accounting applications of these different cost concepts.

SESSION **3 The use of marginal costs, cost-volume-profit analysis and contribution analysis in management decisions**

Introduction

Upon completion of Session 3, you are expected to be able to:

- build upon your understanding of cost behaviour gained from the previous two sessions to explain and use the concept of contribution
- calculate break-even points, the margin of safety, target profit or revenue, profit/volume ratios and the contribution to sales ratio for the single product situation
- prepare traditional and contribution based break-even and profit/volume charts
- understand the limitations of contribution analysis and cost-volume-profit analysis
- determine the profit maximising production plan, where there is limited demand and one limiting factor (i.e., a limitation in the availability of a production resource).

3.1 The concept of contribution

In the previous two sessions of this unit, we discussed the behaviour of different types of fixed and variable costs. This understanding is very useful because we can now discuss the concept of contribution which is defined as follows in a simple one product situation:

Selling price per unit – variable costs per unit = contribution per unit

Contribution per unit means quite literally the contribution that every unit sold makes towards first of all covering fixed costs and then towards earning profit. Once you understand this concept, you will find it very useful in all sorts of short-term decision making. Take the example below of a financial services company which offers a 'one price' service completing tax returns and calculating any tax due, which it refers to as Tax Treats. Next year the company plans to provide or sell 1,000 Tax Treats for £100 each. The company's contribution operating statement will look as follows:

	Per unit (£)	Total (£)
Sales (1,000 Tax Treats)	100	100,000
Variable costs	(60)	(60,000)
Contribution	40	40,000
Fixed costs		(30,000)
Net profit		10,000

From this statement we can see that a contribution of £40,000 is made which literally *contributes to covering fixed costs of £30,000, leaving a net profit of £10,000.*

3.2 Calculating break-even points, the margin of safety, target profit or revenue, profit/volume ratios and the contribution to sales ratio for the single product situation

Breaking even

Make sure you remember this apparently simple definition as it is key to understanding cost behaviour.

Break even occurs when there is neither a profit nor a loss. This is referred to as the **break-even point (BEP)**

Keeping with the case of the single product company above, the management team will be interested to know the minimum number of Tax Treats it needs to sell to avoid making a loss. In other words, how many Tax Treats does it need to sell to break even?

Activity 3.1

How many Tax Treats do you think will need to be sold in order to break even?

Spend about ten minutes answering this.

Feedback

Think about the logic you need to apply in answering this question.

As noted, break even occurs when there is neither a profit nor a loss. In this case, as the fixed costs are £30,000, that much contribution is required in order to break even. This is shown below.

Contribution operating statement – the break-even point

	Per unit £	Total £
Sales (750 Tax Treats)	100	75,000
Variable costs	(60)	(45,000)
Contribution	40	30,000
Fixed costs		(30,000)
Net profit		NIL

The figure of 750 Tax Treats needed to break even can be arrived at as follows. Each Tax Treat makes a contribution of £40, so, to cover fixed costs of £30,000, we divide £30,000 by the £40 contribution per unit to give us the figure of 750 Tax Treats necessary to break even.

Once the company has succeeded in selling enough Tax Treats to provide £30,000 contribution (i.e., 750 Tax Treats), then each extra Tax Treat service the company sells will provide a contribution of £40 (= £100 – £60) to profits. If 751 Tax Treats were sold, the contribution statement would be as shown in the following table.

Contribution operating statement

	Per unit £	Total £
Sales (751 Tax Treats)	100	75,100
Variable costs	(60)	(45,060)
Contribution	40	30,040
Fixed costs		(30,000)
Net profit		40

Once the break-even point has been reached and all costs, including fixed costs, have been covered, any extra contribution generated is additional profit.

You do not need to produce different operating statements to calculate net profit or loss for any level of sales. All you need do is to calculate how much the sales volume is above (profit) or below (loss) the break-even point and multiply the answer by the contribution per unit. So at 1,000 units, the profit is 1,000 – 750, that is 250 units × £40 = £10,000.

With this simple technique, you can calculate, for instance, the effect of the sales achieved by following several different selling or marketing strategies on an organisation's profits. This will hold good as long as the fixed costs remain constant. It is often called the **contribution to sales ratio principle**. In the case of the financial services company, it can be calculated as:

$$\frac{\text{Contribution per Tax Treat}}{\text{Sales revenue per Tax Treat}} \times 100 = \frac{£40}{£100} \times 100 = 40\%$$

This principle is applied in the following activity.

Activity 3.2 ....

What would be the resulting contribution if sales of Tax Treats rose to 1,600 units, using the contribution to sales ratio approach?

Spend about ten minutes on this.

Feedback ....

Using the ratio approach (contribution = 40% x sales, as you can see in the earlier contribution operating statement):

1,600 x £100 x 40% = £64,000

Using the contribution per unit approach:

1,600 x £40 = £64,000

The contribution to sales ratio is a useful concept because it provides a simple and immediate guide to profit or surplus levels and helps to identify activities that have the highest and lowest contribution per unit and their impact on reported profits and losses or surpluses and deficits. This is particularly important and useful when an organisation has more than one operation or activity, each with different cost profiles.

Break even analysis is an accounting technique that identifies the level at which an activity has no profit and no loss, no surplus or deficit. This activity level, as stated earlier, is generally referred to as the break-even point (BEP) and may be expressed as a value in £ or in units. In Activity 3.1, we calculated the BEP of a financial services company. At a level of £75,000 sales, the company had no profit and no loss because its total revenue was exactly equal to its total costs for that level of activity. Alternatively, its contribution was exactly equal to its fixed costs. Given this, there is a particularly simple way of calculating the BEP for any operation or activity.

'This new grocery store is divided into two sections: organic and things I can afford.'

The break-even point

The BEP is determined by simply dividing the total fixed costs by the contribution per unit.

For the financial services company this would give, as we have already seen:

$$\frac{\text{Total fixed costs}}{\text{Contribution per unit}} = \frac{£30,000}{£40} = 750 \text{ Tax Treats}$$

You can also do this using the contribution to sales ratio. The answer is then in terms of the sales revenue required to break even. In our example, the contribution to sales ratio is 40 per cent and the formula is therefore:

$$\frac{\text{Total fixed costs}}{\text{Contribution to sales ratio}}$$

$$= \frac{£30,000}{40\% \text{ (i.e., 0.40 for the purposes of this calculation)}}$$

$$= £75,000 \text{ sales revenue required}$$

Look back at Activity 3.1 feedback to check this for yourself.

Margin of safety

This indicates by how much sales may decrease before a loss occurs. This can be expressed as follows:

Percentage margin of safety

$$= \frac{\text{Expected sales } \textit{minus} \text{ break-even sales}}{\text{Expected sales}} \times 100$$

Let us look at the original financial services company example from earlier in this session as in Activity 3.1. We are provided with the following data:

	Per unit £	Total £
Sales (1,000 Tax Treats)	100	100,000
Variable costs	(60)	(60,000)
Contribution	40	40,000
Fixed costs		(30,000)
Net profit		10,000

750 units are required to break even, thus:

$$\text{The margin of safety is: } \frac{1,000 - 750 \text{ units}}{1,000 \text{ units}} \times 100 = 25\%$$

Now suppose that we wanted to earn a particular **target profit**. How would we calculate the number of units we would have to sell? Remember from earlier in this session that 'contribution' means contribution to fixed costs and profit. So let us apply this to the Tax Treats example above and assume that we want to earn a profit of £15,000.

$$\frac{\text{Target profit } £15,000 + \text{Fixed costs } £30,000}{\text{Contribution per unit } £40}$$
$$= £45,000/£40 = 1,125 \text{ units or Tax Treats}$$

The same answer is obtained by dividing the desired profit of £15,000 by the contribution per unit of £40 to give 375 units and by then adding this to the break even quantity of 750 units to give 1,125 units.

3.3 Preparing contribution-based break-even and profit/volume graphs/charts

Now let us look at the use of graphs or charts to understand more fully the concepts we have just covered.

Profit/volume graphs

We can draw a profit/volume graph to display the relationship between profits and sales/volume. The y (vertical) axis will show profits/loss at different volume levels which are mapped on the x (horizontal) axis.

The figure below shows a profit/volume graph for our financial services company which provides the Tax Treat service.

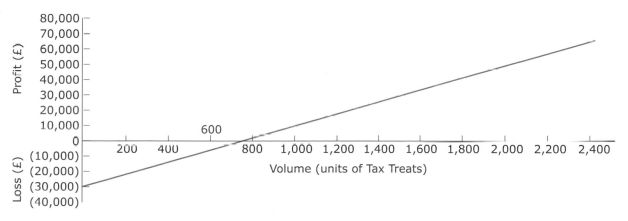

Figure 8 Profit/volume graph for the financial services company

You can see from the graph that break even occurs at 750 units as we calculated in Section 3.2. In fact, from this graph, you can measure the profit/loss at different activity levels. At volumes beyond the break-even point, profits will be made. When the volume is zero, there is a loss equal to the fixed costs.

Another type of graph, the break-even chart, is designed to let you calculate the break-even point. We will illustrate this in the following example.

Contribution-based break-even charts

You are given the details below for Product A.

Product A	£-per unit
Sales price	**50**
Material costs	15
Labour costs	10
Variable overheads	5
Total variable cost	30
Fixed costs: assuming 10,000 units produced and sold. Fixed costs are £50,000	5
Total cost: this is actually total absorption cost, a concept we will explore more fully in Session 4.	**35**

Now let us look at the break-even chart mapping these data.

The horizontal axis is volume (as before in the Tax Treat example) while the vertical axis measures cost and revenues. The first line to note is the fixed cost line. This is a horizontal line because fixed costs do not vary with volume. Then the total costs line can be drawn. When the volume is zero, the total costs will just be the fixed costs of £50,000. When volume is 5,000 units, the total costs will be £50,000 + £30 × 5,000 = £200,000.

Finally, the revenue line can be drawn. This starts at £NIL when no units are sold and will rise at the rate of £50 per unit. When 5,000 units are sold, the revenue will be £250,000. Note again where the break-even point occurs. Above the break-even point, profits are made: the difference between revenue and total costs. Below the

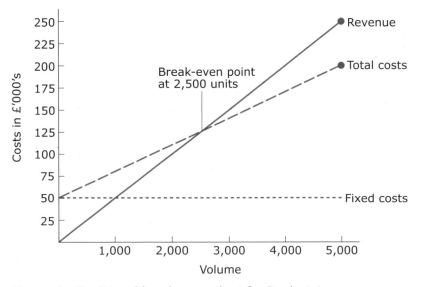

Figure 9   Traditional break-even chart for Product A

break-even point, costs exceed revenue and a loss is made. Note that to find the profit from the graph you have to find the revenue and the costs, then subtract the costs from the revenue.

Hopefully, you will agree that using such charts can provide a useful graphical representation of cost and revenue behaviour at different volumes.

The techniques covered in this session are really powerful to use in short-term decision making. However, we now need to consider some of the limitations of break-even analysis.

3.4 The limitations of break-even analysis

Break-even analysis does suffer from the following limitations which need to be kept in mind.

- The relationships between the variables are assumed to remain constant.
- Profits (or surpluses in a not-for-profit organisation) are calculated on a marginal costing basis.
- Linearity is assumed, that is, variable costs and sales revenues change in direct proportion and in the same direction as changes in activity levels.
- The relevant range needs to be considered. This is explained in more detail below.
- A constant sales mix or single product or service is assumed.

We shall now look at each of these assumptions in a little more detail.

The relationships between the variables are assumed to remain constant

It is normally assumed that, apart from the particular variables you are considering, all the other variables (including production methods, production efficiency, sales price, sales mix and sales levels) will remain constant throughout the analysis process. The problems presented by such an assumption can easily be identified, given the effect on sales revenues and costs of changes in other variables at this level of sales.

Importantly, if variables relating to those circumstances change, a new break-even analysis is needed.

This means that a break-even analysis will apply only to a given set of circumstances. In practice, organisations can prepare several analyses for different sets of circumstances. For example, in the case of our financial services company, break even could be calculated for a range of different sales prices for Tax Treats. (Of course, it would need to take account of the likely response of customers to changes in selling price.) If anticipated changes do not happen but other changes do, a new analysis or, indeed, new sets of analyses, will be needed.

Profits are calculated on a marginal costing basis

This means that it is assumed that all the fixed costs for a period will be charged to profit and loss as expenses for that period. You will learn in Session 4 of this unit that this is not the case under absorption costing.

Linearity

Break-even analysis assumes that revenue and costs are directly proportional to output. Continuing with the original Tax Treats example, if you provide and sell 10 additional Tax Treats, costs rise by ten times (£60) and sales revenue rises by ten times (£100). In other words, it assumes that the unit variable cost and the selling price are constant irrespective of the level of activity.

Relevant range

This means that figures may be appropriate only for decisions taken within a relevant range in which variable costs and revenue per unit and total fixed costs remain constant. If an organisation wants to consider a level of activity beyond the relevant range, it needs to ascertain whether any of the costs (both variable cost per unit and total fixed costs) or revenue per unit will change.

Constant sales mix or single product/service

This limitation of break-even analysis arises because it is assumed that either a single product is sold or, where a range of products is sold, that a constant **sales mix** will be achieved. When there is a range of goods or services with different contributions per unit, *average* variable costs and *average* revenues for the mix may be necessary. Of course, averages can hide a lot!

3.5 Limiting factor analysis

Limiting factor analysis is also known as **key factor** analysis.

Every organisation is in a situation where some of its resources are limited and it may not be able to do all the activities it would like. Important managerial decisions have to be made about the use of resources to ensure efficiency, effectiveness and value for money. The key factor in such decisions is the scarcity of *one* of the resources concerned.

An example of limiting factor analysis

An up-market catering company provides two standard ready two course meals, for which it charges identical prices to a public sector organisation. The catering company's fixed costs for these meals are £20,000. The contribution per unit of ready meal X is £6 and it is £4 for ready meal Y. Since the ready meals are provided and sold in equal amounts, the average contribution is £5 and the break-even sales volume is 4,000 units (fixed costs of £20,000 ÷ £5 contribution per unit). As the two ready meals are provided in equal volumes, 4,000 units overall represent 2,000 units of X and 2,000 units of Y. The catering company would prefer on financial grounds to provide only ready meal X because it has the higher contribution. Can it do this?

Resources may be limited. There may be a limit, for example, imposed by a scarce ingredient, such as the spice saffron. The decision about which product to provide must take any such resource limits (or constraints) into account. The underlying principle in such decisions is:

When any resource is scarce, management should, maximise the contribution per unit of that scarce resource.

Suppose that, in this case, the scarce resource is skilled staff. This is represented by the hours that can be worked. There are only 8,000 staff hours available per year. Ready meal X consumes two staff hours per unit and ready meal Y consumes only one hour per unit. In this case, X produces £3 contribution per staff hour (£6 ÷ 2 hours) and Y produces £4 contribution per staff hour (£4 ÷ 1 hour).

Activity 3.3 ....

Assuming there is no limit on demand, how much of each ready meal do you think the catering company should provide?

Spend five minutes thinking about this.

Feedback ....

With only 8,000 hours available, concentrating on ready meal X will produce £24,000 total contribution and ready meal Y will produce £32,000 total contribution. Hence, because of the limit on skilled staff hours, the business should provide ready meal Y rather than ready meal X. Where there is one limiting factor, organisations should maximise contribution by producing or providing as much as possible of the product or service with the highest contribution per unit of limiting factor.

Applying these principles to a manufacturing environment where the aim is to maximise profit, there is limited demand and one limiting factor, the same approach should be used. Specifically, contribution per unit of limiting factor should be calculated. Products should then be ranked according to contribution per unit of limiting factor. This is shown in the following example (adapted from Drury, 2008, p. 198).

A company produces three components, X, Y and Z and faces a situation where machine hours are scarce in that they are limited to 12,000 hours. Demand is also limited for the components. You are presented with the following information:

	Component X	Component Y	Component Z
Contribution per unit	£12	£10	£6
Machine hours required	6 hours	2 hours	1 hour
Contribution per machine hour	£2	£5	£6
Ranking	3	2	1
Maximum demand	6,000 units	2,000 units	6,000 units

So, given these rankings, the company can allocate its total 12,000 scarce machine hours in accordance with these rankings.

The company should manufacture the three components as follows:

	Units	Machine hours used	Contribution per machine hour £	Total contribution £
Component Z	6,000	6,000	6	36,000
Component Y	2,000	4,000	5	20,000
Component X	333	1,998	2	3,996
Total		11,998		59,996

In allocating its total 12,000 scarce machine hours as above, two hours (12,000 – 11,998) are left unused because another full unit of component X can not be produced.

Summary

Now that you have completed this session, you should be able to explain and use the concept of contribution and calculate break-even points, the margin of safety, target profit or revenue, profit/volume ratios and the contribution to sales ratio for the single product situation. Additionally, you should be able to prepare traditional and contribution based break-even and profit/volume charts and appreciate the limitations of break-even analysis. You should also be able to use contribution analysis to solve simple limiting factor problems. Of course, it is one thing to adopt an internal focus on costs alone, but costs also have an impact on prices charged for goods or services.

SESSION **4 Absorption costing as an alternative to marginal costing**

Introduction

Upon completion of Session 4 you are expected to be able to:

- explain the different treatments of direct and indirect costs
- describe the procedures involved in determining production overhead absorption rates
- allocate and apportion production overheads to cost centres using an appropriate basis
- reapportion service cost centre costs to production cost centres (using the reciprocal method) where service cost centres work for each other as well as for production cost centres
- select, apply and discuss appropriate bases for calculating absorption rates
- calculate and explain the under- and over-absorption of overheads
- demonstrate and discuss the effect of absorption and marginal costing on inventory valuation and profit determination
- calculate profit or loss using absorption and marginal costing
- reconcile the profits or losses calculated using absorption and marginal costing
- describe the advantages and disadvantages of absorption and marginal costing
- calculate direct, variable and full costs of products, services and activities using overhead absorption rates to trace indirect costs to cost units
- explain the use of cost information in pricing decisions, including marginal cost pricing and the calculation of 'full cost' based prices to generate a specified return on sales or investment.

In this session, we shall examine the absorption and marginal costing approaches to ascertaining the cost of a product or service.

4.1 Absorption costing

As its name implies, the absorption costing approach seeks to absorb all the production costs, whether fixed or variable, direct or indirect into a given cost object. The way in which this is done is described in the following sections.

Dealing with direct costs is relatively straightforward, but the **allocation** and **apportionment** of indirect costs can be a more complex process, frequently involving judgement.

The purpose of deriving an absorption rate for a production department is to charge each product with a share of the production department's overhead costs (based on its consumption of the department's resources). There is no single method for calculating absorption rates. Management decides, in conjunction with the accountants, what is applicable in a particular set of circumstances and uses a consistent basis. The bases used for absorbing indirect costs into product units include:

- direct labour hours
- direct production hours/machine hours
- units produced
- percentage of sales value
- percentage of direct cost
- activity consumption (activity based costing (ABC) is covered in Unit 3 of this module).

Once defined, the process of determining direct costs is straightforward. The real challenge comes with allocating the indirect costs.

Suppose the marginal cost of making a door is £112, where the marginal cost is the sum of the variable costs:

Cost card – Door	£
Material 20 kg @ £4/kg	80
Labour 4 hours @ £6/hour	24
Production overhead allocated at the rate of 4 machine hours @ £2/hour	8
Marginal cost	112

However, these are not all the costs you would incur if you were making doors on a commercial basis. Other costs might include factory rent, heating and cooling the factory, cleaning and maintenance, warehousing and storage of materials and production administration. The doors could not be made without these costs. Marginal costing includes only variable costs, and the costs just listed would normally be thought of as fixed costs. Indeed, these costs would be known as fixed production overheads and unless some account is taken of them, the cost of items produced is likely to be understated.

However, it is more difficult to account for fixed costs than it is for variable direct costs, where the extra cost of making an extra unit can be directly measured.

One approach to dealing with this problem is to work out an overhead absorption rate as follows.

Let us assume that the fixed overhead production costs for a period were £500, and that in that period ten doors were produced. A fair fixed overhead cost to include in the cost of manufacturing each door might be £50. The fixed overhead absorption rate per unit can be worked out as follows:

$$\frac{\text{Fixed costs in period}}{\text{Units produced in period}}$$

Here the absorption rate is £50 per unit, and this amount would be added to the marginal cost per unit, to give the total absorption cost per unit.

Cost card – Door	£
Material 20 kg @ £4/kg	80
Labour 4 hours @ £6/hour	24
Production overhead allocated at the rate of 4 machine hours @ £2/hour	8
Marginal cost	112
Fixed overheads	50
Total absorption cost	162

The total absorption cost attempts to take into account the cost of all resources needed to make a unit: the marginal cost takes into account only the variable costs. You should note that this simple example is used to illustrate the calculation of a basic absorption rate.

Activity 4.1

Do you think the marginal cost or the total absorption cost gives a better estimate of the cost of an item?

Take five minutes over this activity.

Feedback

It depends. If you wanted to estimate the cost of manufacturing so that you could set your normal selling price, total absorption costing might be better as your selling price should be set high enough to cover all manufacturing costs. However, if you could not sell all you were making at your chosen selling price, and you were offered £120 per door, it would be worth taking that offer as each extra door costs £112. You would make £8 contribution per door.

Over- and under-absorption of overheads

You will remember that we introduced the topic of direct versus indirect costs in Sessions 1 and 2 of this unit. Assuming that we calculate the indirect costs (or overheads) absorbed by a unit based on actual costs, the calculation presents little difficulty. However, in many businesses the cost of production needs to be established before the end of the accounting period, for example, in order to quote selling prices which recover all anticipated costs. In these circumstances, it is necessary to estimate the future level of production activity and the indirect costs (or overheads): in other words, to prepare a plan or budget.

Budgets are used to implement plans but they must be checked against actual data to ensure that they are reliable and valid. We will cover budgeting in Unit 4.

Therefore, at the end of an accounting period, the actual costs and the volume of activity have to be checked against the plan. If the costs are incorrect, the future levels need to be revised to reflect the latest information. If the level of activity differs from the plan, we must adjust for an under-recovery or over-recovery of indirect costs (or overheads). This under- or over-absorption will need to be shown in the management accounting reports. This principle can be illustrated as follows.

	Plan	Actual
Activity level in units	10,000	10,560
Indirect costs	£76,000	£77,340

As can be seen from the above figures, the planned absorption of indirect costs is £7.60 per unit (i.e., £76,000 divided by 10,000 units).

Because the level of activity was greater than planned, there was an over-absorption of indirect costs of £4,256 (£7.60 × 560 units). In other words, we have charged an additional £4,256 to the units produced and, therefore, understated net profit by the same amount.

An opposite effect on profit also arises from the under-estimate of indirect costs. We must deduct £1,340 (£77,340 – £76,000) from profit for that reason. Overall, however, we have understated profit by £2,916 (i.e., £4,256 – £1,340).

In this example, the basis of allocating indirect costs (or overheads) was the number of units produced, but similar problems arise and corrective principles are used whichever method of indirect cost allocation is adopted.

4.2 Marginal costing

Marginal cost is the cost of supplying one more unit (be it a good or a service). It would not be incurred if no more units were supplied. You can check whether something is a marginal cost by asking the question: 'Does the total cost change as the level of activity changes by one unit?' If the answer is 'Yes', the cost forms part of the marginal cost; if it is 'No', the cost is not part of the marginal cost.

Activity 4.2 ....

Use the test question above to decide which of the following is a marginal cost:

(a) petrol used by a taxi

(b) coal consumed by a power station

(c) tyres used by racing cars.

Take five minutes to reflect on this activity.

Feedback ....

The answer is, of course, all three. As the activity changes, so do the costs.

Interestingly, although accounting standards require companies to use absorption costing in preparing financial statements for external users, many companies also use marginal costing for internal purposes, because it may be more appropriate for particular aspects of short-term decision making such as deciding whether to accept a one-off order.

Marginal costing is concerned with the behaviour of costs at different levels of activity and it distinguishes between variable and fixed costs. It contrasts with absorption costing which we covered earlier in this session in that only the variable costs are allocated to a cost object. The fixed costs are treated separately. A summary of a marginal costing statement is shown in the following table. Note the use of the concept of 'contribution', which was discussed in Session 3 of this unit. This concept is crucial to the decision making applications of marginal costing.

A marginal costing statement

	Product A £	Product B £	Product C £	Total £
Sales revenue	64,700	83,500	51,400	199,600
Variable costs	(42,900)	(56,100)	(32,800)	(131,800)
Contribution	21,800	27,400	18,600	67,800
Fixed costs				(46,600)
Profit				21,200

Marginal costing enables the impact of changes in volume (i.e., level of output) on contribution and on profit to be calculated readily.

In this example, the contribution from A is £21,800, from B is £27,400 and from C is £18,600, making a total of £67,800. From this we deduct the fixed costs to arrive at a profit of £21,200. No attempt has been made to allocate or absorb the fixed costs of £46,600 into the cost of the three products. The contribution in a business provides the pool of funds out of which the fixed costs have to be met. Any residue will be the profit or, in the event of a deficit, the result will be a loss.

The principal advantage of marginal costing over absorption costing is that it enables the impact of changes in volume on contribution and on profit to be calculated readily as will be demonstrated in the next section.

4.3 Why two contrasting approaches to costing?

It is important to have a clear understanding of the differences between absorption and marginal costing. Absorption costing can give misleading results when the volume of activity changes. The following table shows how absorption costing might lead to inappropriate decisions if it were to be used for decision making.

An example of absorption costing

	Range A £	Range B £	Range C £	Total £
Sales revenue	200,000	300,000	500,000	1,000,000
Absorbed costs: direct and indirect	(230,000)	(290,000)	(460,000)	(980,000)
Net profit/(loss)	(30,000)	10,000	40,000	20,000

The absorbed costs in this statement are the direct product costs plus the allocation and apportionment of the indirect costs (both fixed and variable). Ranges (product or service) B and C are profitable but A is losing £30,000. At a superficial level, the common sense answer is to discontinue A. In fact, as will be shown, it would be the wrong decision.

Before making any decisions about whether to continue producing a product or providing a service, you need to examine the position in greater depth and classify the costs into fixed and variable components. In other words, you need to take a marginal costing approach to assess the position. The figures can be represented as follows in terms of the contribution each range is making to the overall net profit.

Classifying fixed and variable costs

	Range A £	Range B £	Range C £	Total £
Sales revenue	200,000	300,000	500,000	1,000,000
Less: variable costs	(150,000)	(220,000)	(330,000)	(700,000)
Contribution	50,000	80,000	170,000	300,000
Less: fixed costs				(280,000)
Net profit				20,000

This is much more helpful. All we have done is use the same figures but have broken them down into variable and fixed costs. The contribution from each product has been calculated but no attempt has been made to allocate the fixed costs. The net profit remains the same.

We can now use marginal cost analysis to see what would happen if Range A were discontinued. Assuming that there are no changes to the fixed costs, the position would appear as in the following table.

Marginal cost analysis

	Range B £	Range C £	Total £
Sales revenue	300,000	500,000	800,000
Less: variable costs	(220,000)	(330,000)	(550,000)
Contribution	80,000	170,000	250,000
Less: fixed costs			(280,000)
Net loss			(30,000)

If the business discontinued Range A, it would suffer a loss of £30,000. This is explained by the loss of contribution of £50,000, which 'converts' the original net profit of £20,000 into a net loss of £30,000.

The decision to discontinue Range A would not be sensible. Management needs to address how contributions can be increased or, alternatively, the cost structure reduced, or what could be offered in place of Range A that would improve the position. In the long run, it *might* be possible to reduce fixed costs but, by definition, this is not feasible in the short run.

The advantage of absorption costing is that the total cost of a unit of output is established and can be directly related to the revenue generated. Absorption costing is the normal method of valuing inventory and work-in-progress in financial accounts. In terms of disadvantages, there is the problem of allocating and apportioning fixed indirect costs, which can be subjective and lead to different answers depending on the method used. Another problem is that changes in the volume of activity have to be dealt with by calculating over- or under-recovery of (fixed) indirect costs.

In contrast, marginal costing recognises the effect of changing volumes on the total cost and avoids the sometimes arbitrary method of allocating fixed indirect costs. However, too much of a focus on marginal costing can lead to a danger of not recognising the full impact of fixed costs. In this sense, absorption costing has the advantage.

One way of overcoming the disadvantages of each method is to analyse cost data in terms of direct and indirect as well as variable and fixed. This means that the costs in an organisation can be evaluated on both an absorption cost basis and a marginal cost basis.

It could be argued that absorption costing is appropriate when the level of activity is reasonably stable but, where the volume is less predictable, marginal costing is more appropriate. This is especially so when there is spare capacity and opportunities arise to use some of the capacity at a revenue level that just exceeds marginal cost. In those circumstances, it is often good practice to use spare capacity as long as some contribution is being made to fixed costs and to generating profits.

4.3.1   Absorption and marginal costing

An absorption costing approach assumes that all indirect production costs can be allocated to individual units of production. As you have seen, there is a variety of ways in which indirect costs can be allocated to units of production to arrive at a total cost per unit but, using an absorption costing approach, the total cost of any unit produced will include direct and indirect costs (both fixed and variable). When preparing an income statement, using an absorption costing approach, the cost of sales figure will include all the direct and indirect costs (fixed and variable) associated with producing the unit. The cost of sales figure is calculated using a figure for closing inventory and the value of the closing inventory will be calculated using direct and indirect costs (fixed and variable).

> **Cost of sales**
>
> For example, Kites Ltd sells toy kites. Kites Ltd starts its financial year with 100 toy kites in inventory and buys in 1,750 toy kites. At the end of the financial year, Kites has 250 unsold kites remaining in inventory. The cost of sales figure will be the cost of 100 + 1,750 – 250 = 1,600 kites.

When preparing the absorption costing financial statements, indirect manufacturing/production costs are allocated to units of production in the cost of sales calculation. The direct and indirect selling, distribution and marketing costs and any other non-production costs are shown separately, after the gross profit. This is illustrated in Figures 10 and 11.

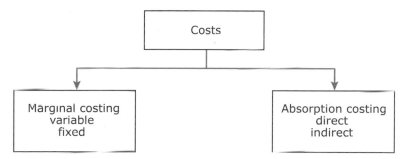

Figure 10 Alternative approaches to cost management

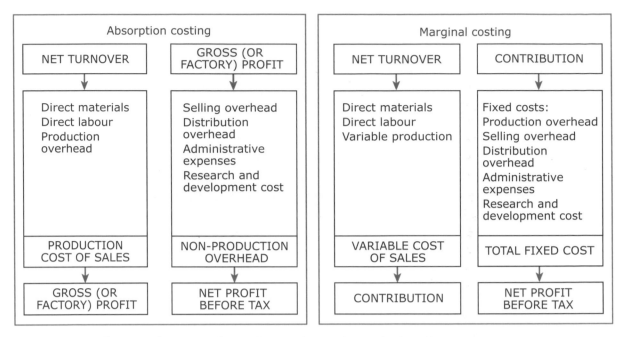

Figure 11   Differences between absorption costing and marginal costing

When using absorption costing in this way, a first in, first out (FIFO) inventory valuation method is assumed. FIFO is the term given to the way in which the inventory is recorded when sold to customers. In FIFO, the first item of inventory received by the business is deemed to be the first issued.

Activity 4.3

A small manufacturing company uses an absorption costing system in which unit costs are calculated on a monthly basis, using FIFO, so that a new absorption rate for indirect costs is calculated each month by dividing the costs incurred during that month by the production in the month. The data for January and February are as follows:

Number of units	January	February
Opening inventory	0	5,000
Production	20,000	30,000
Sales	15,000	28,000

Direct production costs – £ per unit	January	February
Materials	5	5
Labour	4	4

Indirect production costs (manufacturing overheads) are £60,000 each month. The company considers these to be effectively fixed costs. Indirect marketing costs are 20 per cent of sales revenue. The selling price of each unit produced is £25. You are asked to prepare the absorption costing income statements for January and February.

Spend about 15 minutes on this.

Feedback   ....

In order to prepare the absorption costing income statements for January and February, the first step is to calculate the revenue and the cost of sales figures for each month. Closing inventory for January is 5,000 units (production less sales units, that is, 20,000 – 15,000) and closing inventory for February is 7,000 units (opening inventory plus production less sales units, that is, 5,000 + 30,000 – 28,000).

		January				February
	Units	£'000	£'000	Units	£'000	£'000
Sales	15,000		375	28,000		700
Cost of sales						
Opening inventory	0	0		5,000	60	
Materials	20,000	100		30,000	150	
Labour	20,000	80		30,000	120	
Indirect production costs	20,000	60		30,000	60	
Closing inventory	5,000	(60)		7,000	(77)	
Cost of sales			(180)			(313)
Gross profit			195			387
Marketing costs (20% of sales revenue)			(75)			(140)
Profit			120			247

January's closing inventory adjustment is total production costs £240,000 ÷ 20,000 (units produced) x 5,000 units = £60,000. In January, 20,000 units were produced so the indirect production costs were absorbed by 20,000 units (£3 per unit), resulting in a total unit production cost of £12 per unit.

February's closing inventory adjustment is total production costs £330,000 ÷ 30,000 (units produced) x 7,000 units = £77,000. In February, 30,000 units were produced and the indirect production costs were absorbed over 30,000 units (£2 per unit), resulting in a total production cost of £11 per unit.

An absorption costing approach rewards production activity by including a share of the fixed costs in closing inventory, thus rolling them over into the next period. Marginal costing does not do this, so that profit corresponds with sales rather than production. You should note that marginal costing takes a different approach, as it focuses on contribution, that is, sales less variable costs. In a marginal costing approach, only variable costs are taken into account when calculating the cost of sales and the closing inventory adjustment. Using the same information in Activity 4.3, we can prepare a contribution costing income statement:

	January £'000	January £'000	February £'000	February £'000
Sales		375		700
Opening inventory			45	
Materials	100		150	
Labour	80		120	
Closing inventory	(45)		(63)	
Variable cost of sales		(135)		(252)
Marketing costs		(75)		(140)
Contribution		165		308
Indirect production costs		(60)		(60)
Marginal profit		105		248

January's closing inventory adjustment is the variable (direct, in this case) production costs £180,000 ÷ 20,000 (units produced) × 5,000 units = £45,000.

February's closing inventory adjustment is the variable production costs £270,000 ÷ 30,000 (units produced) × 7,000 units = £63,000.

In a marginal costing approach, there may be additional variable costs not associated with production and these need to be included in the calculation of contribution, but not within the cost of sales calculation. Only variable production costs are shown in the cost of sales figure. Inventory valuations and the balance sheet value of closing inventory will be lower in a marginal costing statement.

The absorption costing and marginal costing income statements show different profit figures. This is due to the (fixed) indirect production cost, which is included in the closing inventory adjustment, in the absorption costing approach, and which is carried forward into the next management reporting period. The closing inventory adjustment delays the recording of the total monthly production cost and so, in January, absorption costing reports a higher profit than marginal costing. As the higher reported profit is the result of an accounting adjustment which reverses the following month (the closing inventory adjustment), there is no additional profit being generated and the two profit figures can be reconciled. If there were no closing inventory, then the profit figures would agree.

Reconciliation of absorption costing and marginal costing profits in Activity 4.3.

	January £'000	February £'000
Absorption profit	120	247
Difference in opening inventory	0	15
Difference in closing inventory	(15)	(14)
Marginal profit	105	248

The marginal costing approach recognises all costs in the financial period in which they are incurred. Absorption costing recognises indirect costs in the period in which the goods, or units produced, are sold rather than when the costs are incurred. Accounting standards require that formal financial reports, such as the audited annual report and accounts, show the cost of sales using the absorption costing approach but, from a management accounting perspective, organisations can choose the most appropriate way for their business, in terms of the usefulness of the different accounting statements for them.

4.4 Under-/over-absorption of indirect costs

In Activity 4.3, in the absorption costing statements, all the indirect costs were absorbed into the units produced during each month. This may not always be the case, depending on the absorption rate that an organisation decides to use. For example, using the information in Activity 4.3 for the month of January, assume that the management accountant has decided that the indirect costs will be allocated to a unit on the basis of £2 per unit. Indirect production costs are £60,000 a month, so will be £720,000 a year. The management accountant thinks that 360,000 units will be produced over the year, so the appropriate absorption rate is £2 a unit.

Activity 4.4 ....

Re-work the absorption costing statement for January using an absorption rate of £2 a unit.

Spend ten minutes doing this.

Feedback ....

		January
	Units	**£'000**	**£'000**
Sales	15,000		375
Cost of sales			
Opening inventory	0	0	
Materials	20,000	100	
Labour	20,000	80	
Indirect production costs	20,000	40	
Closing inventory	5,000	(55)	
Cost of sales			(165)
Gross profit			210
Marketing costs			(75)
Profit			135

January's closing inventory adjustment is total production costs £220,000 ÷ 20,000 (units produced) x 5,000 units = £55,000. The indirect production costs were absorbed by 20,000 units (£2 per unit), resulting in a total unit production cost of £11 per unit.

The reconciliation of the above absorption costing profit of £135,000 with the marginal costing profit for January of £105,000 will need to take into account the under-absorption of indirect production costs in January.

Reconciliation of absorption costing and marginal costing profits in January.

	January
	£'000
Absorption profit	135
Difference in opening inventory	0
Difference in closing inventory	(10)
Under-/over-absorption of indirect costs	(20)
Marginal profit	105

An alternative approach is to show the under-absorption of indirect production costs in the absorption costing profit statement itself.

	Units	£'000	January £'000
Sales	15,000		375
Cost of sales			
Opening inventory	0	0	
Materials	20,000	100	
Labour	20,000	80	
Indirect production costs	20,000	40	
Closing inventory	5,000	(55)	
Cost of sales			(165)
Gross profit			210
Marketing costs			(75)
Under-absorption of indirect costs			(20)
Profit			115

Activity 4.5 ....

Now reconcile the absorption costing profit of £115,000 with the marginal costing statement profit of £105,000.

Spend a few minutes on this.

Feedback ....

Reconciliation of absorption costing and marginal costing profits in Activity 4.4.

	January £'000
Absorption profit	115
Difference in opening inventory	0
Difference in closing inventory	(10)
Under-/over-absorption of indirect costs	0
Marginal profit	105

The difference between the two profit figures arises from the difference in the closing inventory.

4.5 Allocation of indirect costs to production and service departments

Manufacturing organisations have both production and service departments. Service departments provide support services to other areas of the business, for example, a legal department providing legal advice to a sales department, with regard to customer contracts, or a maintenance department maintaining the machines in the production department. All departments, whether production or service, will be incurring overhead costs such as heating, rent or use of the company restaurant. These will be the indirect costs of the organisation. In a full or absorption costing approach, all production-related direct and indirect costs will need to be allocated to units of production. Direct costs are straightforward as they can be linked with particular products. For example, every time a unit is produced a certain value of material is used. Indirect costs are harder to allocate to individual units produced because the amount of resource used may not be conveniently measurable. This is what distinguishes direct costs from many indirect costs. Think of a company producing furniture. What is the best way to allocate the quarterly rental payment for the factory to the individual tables and chairs being produced? Allocating or apportioning the rental costs on the basis of units produced may not be the best solution for arriving at an appropriate total cost. In this case, different products may require different sizes of area in a factory to be produced, so that rental costs might be better allocated on the basis of relative use of factory space. While any allocation method involves a managerial decision about the basis of allocating indirect costs to units produced, there is a general approach that can be used.

The first step in the process is to allocate indirect non-production costs to specific service departments (production indirect costs are obviously allocated to production departments) and after that re-allocate each service department's total indirect costs to production departments. Then, when all the indirect costs have been allocated to production departments, a full cost per unit can be calculated, by apportioning the total of the departmental costs (direct and indirect) among product units.

Activity 4.6 ....

A division within a manufacturing company, which produces domestic appliances such as electric toasters and kettles, has four departments: two service departments, which are Purchasing and Production Administration, and two production departments, Department T (electric toasters) and Department G (electric grills). Annual indirect costs for the division which require allocation to departments are the rent (£210,000) and electricity (£52,500). The management accountant has provided the following information:

	Department T	Department G	Purchasing	Administration
Units produced	12,500	25,000		
Direct costs per unit	£10.00	£15.00		
Direct labour hours	20,000	40,000		
Floor space	2,000m^2	1,000m^2	200m^2	300m^2
Staff employed	11	22	2	5

Using a full cost approach, calculate a total cost per product for Department T and Department G. Use floor space for each department to allocate indirect costs to all departments. Use the units produced by each department to allocate the total indirect costs for each service department to Departments T and G.

Spend about 15 minutes on this.

Feedback ....

	Dept. T £	Dept. G £	Purchasing £	Administration £	Total £
Rent	120,000	60,000	12,000	18,000	210,000
Electricity	30,000	15,000	3,000	4,500	52,500
Total	150,000	75,000	15,000	22,500	262,500
Re-allocate Purchasing	5,000	10,000	(15,000)		0
Re-allocate Administration	7,500	15,000		(22,500)	0
Total indirect costs	162,500	100,000			262,500
Indirect cost per unit	13	4			
Direct cost per unit	10	15			
Total cost per unit	23	19			

The allocation of the indirect costs from service departments to production departments has been done on the basis of units produced by each department and this seems a reasonable approach as Department G is twice the size of Department T and, we might assume, uses more of the Purchasing and Production Administration services than Department G, assuming the products are similar.

The initial allocation of the rent and electricity indirect costs was done on the basis of floor space but here the smaller department (in terms of production), Department T, occupies the larger floor space and so has received a larger allocation of indirect costs, and each toaster then absorbs more indirect costs than each electric grill. The choice of allocation basis affects the final cost per unit and any subsequent decision based on those costs, for example, pricing decisions or assessing the profitability of competing products. For these reasons, it is important that an appropriate basis for initial allocation of indirect costs is chosen. You can judge this for yourself in the following activity.

Activity 4.7 ....

See how the total cost per unit changes when Activity 4.6 is repeated but the number of employees in each department is used to allocate the indirect costs in the first step. As before, use the units produced by each department to allocate the total indirect costs for each service department to Departments T and G.

Spend no more than 15 minutes on this.

Feedback ....

	Dept. T £	Dept. G £	Purchasing £	Administration £	Total £
Rent	57,750	115,500	10,500	26,250	210,000
Electricity	14,437.5	28,875	2,625	6,562.5	52,500
Total	72,187.5	144,375	13,125	32,812.5	262,500
Re-allocate Purchasing	4,375	8,750	(13,125)		0
Re-allocate Administration	10,937.5	21,875		(32,812.5)	0
Total indirect costs	87,500	175,000			262,500
Indirect cost per unit	7	7			
Direct cost per unit	10	15			
Total cost per unit	17	22			

Department G's products now have the higher full cost, as indirect costs per unit under this approach are the same for both types of product.

The choice of allocation and apportionment basis is a management decision, which will involve the management accountant. Such a decision needs to avoid being arbitrary and should aim to take an even-handed approach in determining appropriate rates. The managers of Department T would, no doubt, prefer to have indirect costs allocated on the basis of employees, arguing that it gives a fairer view of the total costs of their product (and makes 'their' product look more profitable). Inevitably, the final decision will involve an element of subjectivity.

4.6 Reciprocal allocation of indirect costs: service departments

A further issue is the allocation of indirect costs when service departments carry out work for each other, for example, the information systems department producing information on employee working hours for the human resource department or the human resource department requiring the services of the in-house lawyer in the legal department for employment contracts. This type of support activity is known as reciprocal support and a reciprocal allocation method is used to allocate indirect costs. This approach allows the allocation method to reflect the mutual nature of inter-departmental activities.

For example, a manufacturing division has four departments. The support departments, Finance Systems (provision of financial and other management information) and Maintenance (maintenance of computer equipment and networks as well as production machinery) provide services to each other as well as to the production departments, Department A and Department B. In this example, indirect costs have already been allocated to the departments.

	Finance Systems (FS) Department	Maintenance (M) Department	Department A	Department B	Total
Indirect costs allocated	£100,000	£500,000	£400,000	£200,000	£1,200,000
Percentage of support work performed by Finance Systems	–	10%	80%	10%	100%
Percentage of support work performed by Maintenance	20%	–	30%	50%	100%

The indirect costs of the two support departments and the reciprocal relationships can be shown as linear equations, as follows:

FS = £100,000 + 0.2M

M = £500,000 + 0.1FS

Total indirect costs to be allocated from FS department to the production departments are the indirect costs allocated plus 20 per cent of the indirect costs of M department. Total indirect costs to be allocated from M department to the production departments are the indirect costs allocated plus 10 per cent of the indirect costs of FS department.

To find FS and M

$$FS = 100,000 + 0.2M \textbf{ Equation (1)}$$

$$M = 500,000 + 0.1FS \textbf{ Equation (2)}$$

Line (see explanation in margin note)

1 $FS = 100,000 + 0.2 (500,000 + 0.1FS)$
2 $FS = 100,000 + 100,000 + 0.02 FS$
3 $FS (1 - 0.02) = 200,000$
4 $FS = 200,000 \div 0.98 = 204,082$
5 $FS = 204,082$
6 Now, substitute 204,082 into $M = 500,000 + 0.1FS$
7 $M = 500,000 + 0.1 (204,082)$
8 $M = 500,000 + 20,408 = 520,408$
9 $M = 520,408$

From Equation (2) we have a formula for M so we substitute this for M in Equation (1) to give a value for FS which can be solved (see Line 1).
We then multiply out the brackets to arrive at Line 2 to arrive at a total FS cost to be allocated of £204,082. (see Lines 3 to 5).
Then, as per Line 6, we substitute 204,082 into M. $M = 500,000 + 0.1FS$.
In Line 7 we then multiply out the brackets and simplify M to arrive at a total M cost to be allocated of £520,408.

Solving these equations gives a complete reciprocated cost for FS department of £204,082 and for M department of £520,408. This is also known as an artificial cost and the calculated figure will be larger than the allocated indirect costs.

The complete reciprocated costs of each support department can be allocated to departments on the basis of the percentage of usage.

	Finance Systems (FS) Department	Maintenance (M) Department	Department A	Department B	Total
	£	£	£	£	£
Indirect costs allocated	100,000	500,000	400,000	200,000	1,200,000
Allocation of Maintenance	104,082	(520,408)	156,122	260,204	0
Allocation of Finance Systems	(204,082)	20,408	163,266	20,408	0
Total after reciprocal allocation	0	0	719,388	480,612	1,200,000

In the table above, the artificial cost for FS has been allocated as follows:

		£
To Maintenance department	10% × £204,082	20,408
To Department A	80% × £204,082	163,266
To Department B	10% × £204,082	20,408
Total		204,082

Check the allocation of Maintenance department using the same approach.

The reciprocal approach is an accurate way to solve the problem of inter-departmental activity with relation to indirect costs. However, it still relies on a management decision regarding the percentage of costs to be allocated (the subjective element still exists) and is more complex, although the mathematical solution and final allocation is easily performed by readily available software. The direct way of allocating indirect costs, seen in Activity 4.6, remains a preferred method by many managers, for reasons of simplicity.

4.7 Advantages and disadvantages of different costing approaches

We have looked at absorption costing and marginal costing approaches in a variety of management accounting scenarios. Before moving on to the final topic in this session, carry out the following activity.

Activity 4.8 ....

What are the relative advantages and disadvantages of absorption and marginal costing approaches?

Spend about ten minutes on this activity.

Feedback ....

The subjectivity involved in total absorption costing, in selecting an appropriate allocation method for indirect costs, is a disadvantage as the total cost may be a misstatement or may have been manipulated. On the other hand, knowing the total cost for a unit of production is critical for making pricing decisions and assessing profitability. While marginal costing can be criticised for ignoring fixed costs, or not paying them sufficient attention, knowing the marginal cost of one unit of production and the associated relationship of contribution to fixed costs is useful when considering business development opportunities. If the contribution from existing business activities covers or exceeds the existing fixed costs, then any additional business activity, if there is spare capacity to carry it out, will generate additional contribution, and profits. Marginal costing is useful in short-run decisions, as it focuses on incremental revenue and cost data, by considering how much better off we might be, for example, if we go ahead with a new contract. However, in the long run, companies need to consider total costs.

4.8 Pricing decisions using absorption and marginal costing approaches

One of the disadvantages of using an absorption costing approach can be identified in the context of pricing. The following example illustrates how different total costs arise from different indirect cost allocation bases. (You may wish to refer back to Activities 4.6 and 4.7 here.)

	Total cost – electric toaster £	Total cost – electric grill £
Indirect costs allocated on the basis of floor space	23	19
Indirect costs allocated on the basis of departmental employees	17	22

If a major competitor for kitchen appliances is selling a similar electric toaster at £25, then this competitive price may also have to be adopted by the firm in our example above. The profit margin will vary according to which allocation method is used. This highlights the importance of allocating indirect costs in an appropriately justifiable manner (but you should note that this will still be subjective). With a total cost of £23 and a market-led selling price of £25, the decision may be to discontinue production of electric toasters as, at £2, the profit margin may be too low.

However, once an appropriate allocation method has been chosen, absorption costing is useful when the management accountant wants to use a cost-plus approach in pricing. A **cost-plus price** is the price decided by adding an amount to the costs to arrive at a sales price.

Example

The direct costs of a product are £30 and the allocated indirect costs are £15. The company wants to earn a profit margin of 25 per cent. The profit margin (or return on sales percentage) is calculated as profit ÷ sales × 100.

Total cost of the product is £45. Sales price will be £60, calculated as £45 ÷ 0.75 = £60.

See the following text for how to calculate margin and mark-up.

We can check this: the profit is £15, which is 25 per cent of £60 (sales).

Margin and mark-up

If the profit margin is 25 per cent then the relationship between sales and profit figures is as follows:

Sales	100
Costs	(75)
Profit	25

This gives a profit margin of 25 per cent (profit ÷ sales × 100).

Divide the calculated costs figure by 75 and multiply by 100 to arrive at a sales figure.

Mark-up is the amount added to the costs to arrive at a sales figure.

If mark-up is 20 per cent, then the relationship between sales and profits is as follows:

Sales	120
Costs	(100)
Profit	20

Divide the calculated cost figure by 100 and multiply by 100 + mark-up amount to arrive at a sales figure.

Activity 4.9 ....

The total costs of a product are £60. The company aims to achieve a mark-up of 30%. Calculate the sales price.

Spend only a few minutes on this.

Feedback   ....

£60 x 1.3 = £78

An alternative method to identify a price using a cost-plus approach is to use an expected or pre-determined Return on Investment (ROI). If invested capital is £100,000 and the company wants to achieve a 10 per cent ROI, then £10,000 profit is the minimum profit required. Once a minimum profit figure has been calculated, total costs can be added to the profit figure to give a sales value.

If total costs are £60,000, then £10,000 + £60,000 = £70,000.

The sales value of £70,000 can be divided by the number of units produced to give a selling price per unit.

Cost-plus pricing is straightforward to use and has been a popular approach (Drury, 2008, p. 259). However, adding a percentage amount to costs to arrive at a sales figure takes no account of the response from customers and competitors to the price. Pricing decisions cannot consider the internal processes (cost structures) of the producer alone. The price arrived at must be acceptable to customers and match competitors' prices, if the product is to be sold (see Lucas, 1999).

You may like to read this article which was written by a member of the B292 module team, Dr Mike Lucas. See the References section at the end of this unit for the full reference.

In taking account of fixed and variable costs, direct and indirect, a cost-plus approach is considered a long-run approach, because the aim is to cover the total costs of production in the long term. By way of contrast, a short-run, marginal approach takes into account direct and indirect costs, but importantly, only variable not fixed costs. A marginal costing approach may be appropriate in certain circumstances for short-run business decisions. Suppose a company is offered a three month contract which can be fulfilled without any additional expenditure on fixed costs: then pricing the contract to cover the variable or incremental costs that will be incurred in taking on the contract is recommended. As long as there is surplus operating capacity for the contract within the company, then bidding for the contract on a marginal costing approach is appropriate. However, in such cases, a marginal costing approach is only acceptable so long as it does not undermine full cost pricing in the future or with other customers.

Summary

This session has provided an introduction to absorption costing and marginal costing and has explained the effect of these two approaches on inventory valuation and reported profits. Additionally, we have explored the allocation of indirect costs to production and service departments as well as the effect upon pricing decisions of using the two approaches.

In the next session we shall explore the issue of relevant costs.

SESSION **5 Relevant costs**

Introduction

Upon completion of Session 5 you are expected to be able to:

- explain the concept of relevant cost
- calculate the relevant costs for materials, labour and overheads
- calculate the relevant costs associated with non-current assets
- explain and apply the concept of opportunity cost.

To get you started, let us consider the question of what makes costs either relevant or irrelevant. The emphasis in this session is on short-term decision making, but you should note for your future studies that relevant cost is a crucial concept which is also used in capital investment appraisal, or long-term decision making.

5.1 **Relevant and irrelevant costs**

In making a decision, a possible course of action must be compared with at least one other. In examining the implications of cost data for decision making, the most important questions are: 'which costs are relevant?' and 'which costs are not relevant?' How do we classify which is which?

A relevant cost is one that will occur only if the course of action in question is undertaken. In other words, it can be avoided by taking another course of action. Irrelevant costs can be divided into two categories:

- costs that have already been incurred, known as **sunk costs**
- costs that will occur in the future and will be the same no matter which course of action is taken (known as **committed costs**).

Such costs are known as committed costs because they have been committed and so can not be changed.

Additionally, you may be aware of non-cash costs, such as depreciation, which are also irrelevant.

The important thing in decision making is to ignore all irrelevant costs and concentrate on relevant costs.

In general, the procedures for analysing cost data for decision making are:

(1) ignore all sunk costs

(2) ignore all committed costs

(3) use remaining cash costs for decision making purposes (this includes any opportunity costs, as you will see later in this session). Because it is only cash costs that are relevant, ignore non-cash costs.

The decision can then be based on whether the relevant benefits will be greater than the relevant costs. In Session 3 of this unit, you were introduced to the concept that, for simple short-term decisions, the criterion would be to maximise the contribution towards the profit of the company. This is a special case of the principle followed here, namely, that the relevant benefits should exceed the relevant costs of the decision.

Remember that there may also be non-financial factors that will need to be considered but cannot be formulated into financial terms.

It should be stressed that the focus is on cash flows rather than accounting profits. The net benefit is really a net cash flow (hopefully an inflow). Essentially, the process of assessing the relevant costs involves preparing a schedule of relevant cash flows.

5.2 Calculating the relevant costs for materials, labour and overheads

In order to look at the issues involved in calculating the relevant costs for materials, labour and overhead, you should work through the following activity.

Activity 5.1   ....

XYZ Limited is a small specialist manufacturer of components for the car industry. One of the car manufacturers has offered a contract to XYZ Limited for the supply, over the next 12 months, of 800 identical components. The data relating to the production of each component are as follows:

(i)   *Material requirements*:

- 6 kg of material A1 (see Note 1)
- 1 bought-in component (part number 123) (see Note 2)

Note 1: Material A1 is in continuous use by the business and 1,000 kg are currently held by the business. The original cost was £4.70 per kg but it is known that future purchases will cost £5.50 per kg.

Note 2: It is estimated that the component (part number 123) could be bought in for £50 each.

(ii) *Labour requirements.* Each component would require two and a half hours of skilled labour and two and a half hours of semi-skilled labour. A skilled employee is available and is currently paid £14 per hour. A replacement would, however, have to be obtained at a rate of £12 per hour for the work which would otherwise be done by the skilled employee. The current rate for semi-skilled work is £10 per hour and an additional employee could be appointed for this work.

(iii) *General manufacturing costs.* It is XYZ Limited's policy to charge a share of the general costs (rent, heating and so on) to each contract undertaken at the rate of £20 for each machine hour used on the contract. If the contract is undertaken, the general costs are expected to increase by £3,200.

Spare machine capacity is available and each component would require four machine hours. A price of £200 per component has been offered by the potential customer.

Required

(a) Should the contract be accepted? Support your conclusion with appropriate figures to present to management.

(b) What other factors ought management to consider that might influence the decision?

Spend about 20 minutes on this.

Feedback

Cost	£	Explanation
Material A1 (6 x 800 x £5.50)	26,400	The original cost is irrelevant since any inventories used will need to be replaced.
Part no.123 (800 @ £50)	40,000	This is the bought-in cost.
Skilled labour (2,000 @ £12)	24,000	The effective cost is £12 per hour. The existing wage of £14 per hour will be paid in any event: it is a committed cost. The additional cost arising from undertaking the contract is the cost of replacement labour.
Semi-skilled labour (2,000 @ £10)	20,000	
Overheads	3,200	It is only the additional cost that is relevant: the method of apportioning total overheads is not relevant.
Total relevant cost	113,600	
Potential revenue (800 @ £200)	160,000	

Clearly, on the basis of the information available, it would be beneficial for the business to undertake the contract.

(b)   There are many factors to consider in this part of the question, such as whether the replacement for the skilled worker would be able to do the normal work of that person to the necessary standard; whether training would be needed; whether XYZ Limited is confident that the additional skilled and unskilled employees can be made redundant at the end of the contract without cost to the business.

'To cut down on heating costs, we should consider house pooling.'

5.3 Calculating the relevant costs associated with non-current assets

Here we will consider the case of whether to replace a non-current asset, an item of equipment, which is a welding machine in this example (adapted from Seal et al., 2006, pp. 352–5).

> ## 'Relevant costs' of non-current (or fixed) assets
>
> Soaring Wings Ltd is a small manufacturer of high quality hang gliders. The most critical component of a hang glider is its metal frame, which must be very strong and yet very light. The frames are made by welding together tubes of high strength, but lightweight, metal alloys. Most of the welding must be done by hand, but some can be done in an automated process by machine. Pete Fisher, the production manager, has been trying to convince Jim Marker, the company's Managing Director, to purchase a new welding machine from Furimoro Industries, which would cost £200,000. This machine would replace an old welding machine from Byston Ltd that generates a large amount of scrap and waste.
>
> On a recent blustery morning, Pete and Jim happened to drive into the company's car park at the same time. The following conversation occurred as they walked together into the building.
>
> Pete: Morning, Jim. Have you had a chance to look at the specifications on the new welding machine from Furimoro Industries that I gave you last week?
>
> Jim: Are you still pestering me about the welding machine?
>
> Pete: You know it's almost impossible to keep that old Byston welding machine working within tolerances.
>
> Jim: I know, I know. But we're carrying the Byston machine on the books for £140,000.
>
> Pete: That's right. But I've done some investigating, and we could sell it for £90,000 to a plumbing company in town that doesn't require as tight tolerances as we do.
>
> Jim: Pete, that's just brilliant! You want me to sell a £140,000 machine for £90,000 and take a loss of £50,000. Do you have any other great ideas this morning?
>
> Pete: Jim, I know it sounds far-fetched, but we would actually save money buying the new machine.
>
> Jim: I'm sceptical. However, if you can show me the hard facts, I'll listen.
>
> Pete: Fair enough. I'll do it.

Note that the potential loss from selling the old machine is not relevant. The investment that has been made in the old machine is a sunk cost so that the portion of this investment that remains on the company's books (the book value of £140,000) should not be considered in a decision about whether to buy the new machine. You are provided with the following figures. Note that the irrelevance of the book value of the old machine can be verified by the following analysis of the total cost and revenues of keeping the old machine versus purchasing the new one over a period of four years. Note that revenues and costs are assumed for the purpose of this example, unless specified above.

	Keep old machine £	Purchase new machine £	Differential costs and benefits £
Annual sales remain at £2m irrespective of decision	2,000,000	2,000,000	Nil
Variable costs: VC are £180,000 lower if the new machine is used.	(1,380,000)	(1,200,000)	180,000
Cost of new machine		(200,000)	(200,000)
Book value write-off of old machine	(140,000)	(140,000)	Nil
Disposal value of old machine	–	90,000	90,000
	480,000	550,000	Net gain 70,000

The advantage of buying the new machine is based on the cost of £200,000 and the savings in variable costs of £180,000 plus the disposal proceeds of £90,000.

Based on this analysis, Pete persuaded Jim that the new machine was worthwhile as it would cut scrap and re-work costs. The book value of the old machine is irrelevant as, under either course of action, the cost will eventually flow through the income statement as either a loss on disposal or as depreciation. Pete argued, moreover, that the analysis above understated the true advantages of the new machine. This was because, when using the old machine, it was impossible to catch all of the defects and the defective products were sometimes sold to customers. With the new machine, warranty costs should decrease and repeat sales increase.

We will now turn to the subject of **opportunity costs**.

5.4 Opportunity costs

Let us consider the case of Dr Smith. He earns £32,000 a year after tax, working for a chemical company as a junior engineer. He is considering the possibility of leaving the company and starting his own business. To do this, he will have to use all his £50,000 savings that are currently invested at a net (of tax) interest rate of 5 per cent. He estimates that the annual profit from his own business will be at least £40,000 net of tax. Should he start the business?

If he does, he will lose his salary and the interest on his savings. Each of these is an opportunity cost. The overall effect of the decision is thus:

	£
Projected profit from the business	40,000
Opportunity cost of loss of salary	(32,000)
Opportunity cost, loss of interest	(2,500)

Thus, he would be £5,500 better off if he goes ahead with his plan.

Opportunity costs therefore represent the cost of opportunities *foregone as a result of taking one course of action*. These are as relevant as any other costs in decision making and should therefore be built into decisions. Consider the following further examples.

You may be interested to know that this particular notion of opportunity cost forms the underpinning of discounted cash flow (DCF) methods of capital investment appraisal which will be covered in Unit 5.

Relevant costs and non-current assets – the purchase of land

Suppose that a supermarket chain is considering investing a large sum of money in land that may be a site for a future shop. Rather than invest the funds in land, the company could invest the funds in so-called **blue chip shares** (or **top-rated company shares**). If the land is acquired, the opportunity cost will be the investment income that could have been realised if the shares had been purchased.

(Adapted from Seal et al., 2006, p. 39)

You will notice that opportunity cost is not usually recorded explicitly in the accounts of an organisation. However, Seal et al. (2006) note that virtually every alternative has some opportunity cost attached to it and so these costs are useful in the managerial decision making process.

Summary

This session has provided an introduction to relevant costing in general and to the concept as applied to materials, labour and overheads as well as to the case of non-current assets. It has been shown how, in making a decision, a possible course of action must be compared with at least one other. The session also included an explanation and an application of the vital, related concept of opportunity cost. It was shown that opportunity costs are not usually explicitly recorded in the accounts of an organisation. However, most courses of action have some opportunity cost, so an understanding of this concept is vital in managerial decision making.

Unit summary

You have now completed Unit 2 of B292 *Management accounting*. This unit has introduced you to cost analysis for planning and decision making.

By now, you should have an understanding of the different types of costs, costs and decision making, the use of marginal costs, cost-volume-profit analysis and contribution analysis in managerial decisions, the issue of absorption costing versus marginal costing as well as the important concept of relevant costs, including opportunity costs.

Before moving on to Unit 3 of this module, complete the following self-assessed questions. Make sure you check your answers with those provided before you start Unit 3.

Self-assessed Questions

Where appropriate use examples to support your arguments.

Question 1

Mountain Goat Cycles makes a line of panniers – a saddlebag for bicycles. There are two models of panniers – a touring model and a mountain model. Cost and revenue data for the two models of panniers are given here:

	Mountain pannier £	Touring pannier £
Selling price per unit	25	30
Variable cost per unit	10	18
Contribution margin per unit	15	12
Contribution margin (CM) ratio	60%	40%

The factory that makes the panniers is operating at full capacity, with the bottleneck or scarce resource being a particular stitching machine. The mountain pannier requires two minutes of stitching time, and each unit of the touring pannier requires one minute of stitching time. Since this stitching machine already has more work than it can handle, something will have to be cut back. In this situation, which product is more profitable?

You should prove the accuracy of your answer by calculating how much extra contribution margin would be earned if one extra hour of stitching machine time were to become available.

Suggested answer

	Mountain pannier	Touring pannier
Contribution margin per unit (a)	£15.00	£12.00
Time on the stitching machine required to produce one unit (b)	2 minutes	1 minute
Contribution margin per unit of the scarce resource (a)/(b)	£7.50 per minute	£12.00 per minute

Therefore, the touring model should be emphasised as it produces the larger contribution margin in relation to the scarce resource usage.

To verify that the touring model is indeed the more profitable product, suppose an hour of additional stitching time is available and that there are unfilled orders for both products. The additional hour on the stitching machine could be used to make either 30 mountain panniers (60 minutes/2 minutes) or 60 touring panniers (60 minutes/1 minute) with the following consequences:

	Mountain pannier	Touring pannier
Contribution margin per unit	£15.00	£12.00
Additional units that can be processed in one hour	x 30	x 60
Additional contribution margin	£450	£720

Therefore this proves that the touring pannier should be produced in preference to the mountain pannier.

Question 2

Builder Ltd commenced business on 1 January making one product only. The budgeted cost of one unit of the product is as follows:

	£
Direct material	24
Direct labour	16
Variable production overhead	6
Fixed production overhead	10
Total	56

The fixed production overhead figure has been calculated on the basis of a budgeted normal output of 48,000 units per year. Budgeted fixed expenses are incurred evenly over the year.

Selling and distribution expenses are:

Fixed administration expenses   £30,000 per month

Variable selling and distribution costs   20 per cent of the sales value

The selling price is £100 and there was no opening inventory at the beginning of January. The actual numbers of units produced and sold were:

	January units	February units
Production	3,500	4,000
Sales	3,000	4,200

Actual variable costs per unit and fixed costs were as budgeted. Builder Ltd uses a FIFO approach to value closing inventory.

Required

- Prepare income statements for each of the months of January and February using the absorption costing approach.
- Prepare income statements for each of the months of January and February using the marginal costing approach.
- Reconcile the monthly profits from the two different costing approaches.

Suggested answer ....

Absorption costing approach

	Units	£'000	January £'000	Units	£'000	February £'000
Sales	3,000		300	4,200		420
Cost of sales						
Op. inventory	0	0		500	28	
Materials	3,500	84		4,000	96	
Labour	3,500	56		4,000	64	
Variable prod. o'head	3,500	21		4,000	24	
Fixed prod o'head	3,500	35		4,000	40	
Closing inventory	500	(28)		300	(16.8)	
Cost of sales			(168)			(235.2)
Gross profit			132			184.8
Selling exps.			(60)			(84)
Fixed admin. costs			(30)			(30)
Profit			42			70.8

Marginal costing approach

	Units	£'000	January £'000	Units	£'000	February £'000
Sales	3,000		300	4,200		420
Cost of sales						
Op. inventory	0	0		500	23	
Materials	3,500	84		4,000	96	
Labour	3,500	56		4,000	64	
Variable prod. o'head	3,500	21		4,000	24	
Closing inventory	500	(23)		300	(13.8)	
Cost of sales			(138)			(193.2)
Selling exps.			(60)			(84)
Contribution			102			142.8
Fixed admin. costs			(30)			(30)
Fixed prod. costs			(40)			(40)
Profit			32			72.8

Reconcile monthly profits

	January £'000	February £'000
Absorption profit	42	70.8
Difference in opening inventory	0	5
Difference in closing inventory	(a) (5)	(c) (3)
Under-/over-absorption of fixed costs	(b) (5)	(d) 0
Marginal profit	32	72.8

(a) Using absorption costing, fixed production overhead included in January closing stock is: (3,500 units produced – 3,000 units sold) x £10 per unit = £5,000. (This difference will be carried forward to opening stock for February.)

(b) Using absorption costing, fixed production overhead absorbed is 3,500 units x £10 = £35,000; fixed production overhead incurred is £480,000/12 = 40,000. Therefore, under-absorbed overhead = £5,000.

(c) Using absorption costing, fixed production overhead included in February closing stock is: (opening stock 500 units + 4,000 units produced – 4,200 units sold) x £10 = 3,000.

(d) Using absorption costing, fixed production overhead absorbed is 4,000 units x £10 = £40,000; fixed production overhead incurred is £480,000/12 = £40,000. Therefore, no under- or over- absorption of fixed production overhead.

Question 3

You have been approached by a friend who is seeking your advice as to whether he should give up his job as a junior engineering technician, with a current salary of £1,400 per month, and go into business on his own, assembling and selling a component which he has invented. He can obtain the parts required from various manufacturers.

It is very difficult to forecast the sales potential of the component but, after some research, your friend has estimated that sales could be as follows:

(i) Between 600 and 900 units per month if the selling price is £25 per unit.

(ii) Between 900 and 1250 units per month if the selling price is £22 per unit.

The cost of the parts required would be £14 per completed component. However, if more than 1,000 units can be sold each month, a discount of five per cent on all purchases would be received from the supplier of the parts.

Assembly costs would be £6,000 per month for assembly of up to 750 components. Beyond this level of activity, costs would increase to £7,000 per month.

Your friend has already spent £3,000 on development, which he would write off over the first five years of the venture on a straight-line basis.

Required

(a) Calculate, for each of the possible sales levels, whether your friend could expect to benefit by going into business on his own.

(b) Calculate the break-even point of the venture for each of the selling prices.

(c) Advise your friend as to the viability of the venture. State your key considerations both as regards the technique and the data you are using.

Suggested answer

(a)

Selling price	**£25**	**£25**	**£22**	**£22**
Sales volume	600	900	900	1,250
	£	£	£	£
Contribution per unit	11	11	8	8.70
Total contribution	6,600	9,900	7,200	10,875
Assembly costs	6,000	7,000	7,000	7,000
Profit	600	2,900	200	3,875
Salary foregone	1,400	1,400	1,400	1,400
Gain/(loss)	(800)	1,500	(1,200)	2,475

Disregard the development cost of £3,000 as this is a sunk cost.

(b) At a selling price of £25 the BEP for an activity level below 750 units is:

$$\frac{\text{FC } (£6,000) + \text{salary foregone } (£1,400)}{\text{Contribution per unit } (£11)} = 673 \text{ units}$$

Note that, at 751 units, a loss is made since fixed costs increase from £6,000 to £7,000.

At a selling price of £25 per unit and FC of £7,000 the BEP is 764 units (£8,400/£11).

At a selling price of £22 per unit the BEP calculation is:

$$\frac{\text{FC } (£7,000) + \text{salary forgone } (£1,400)}{\text{Contribution per unit } (£8)} = 1,050 \text{ units}$$

As the BEP is above the point at which contribution increases, you must determine the BEP based on a contribution of £8.70 per unit:

BEP = £8,400/£8.70 = 965 units

This is below the point at which contribution increases. Therefore the BEP is 1,000 units. At 999 units a loss is made but at 1,000 units there is a sudden increase in contribution as a result of receiving a discount on all units purchased.

(c) Key considerations:

- important to consider the individual's attitude to risk
- at the lower level of potential sales level, the individual will be worse off while at the higher level the individual will be better off
- decision will depend on how confident the individual is regarding the estimated sales volume exceeding the BEPs specified in (b)
- before making a decision, longer-term prospects for the venture and the present job also should be considered
- the individual's attitude to self-employment relative to the alternative employment should be considered
- assumptions of cost-volume-profit analysis to be spelt out and evaluated (e.g., relationships between variables are linear, variables do not change in the very short term, etc.).

Question 4

Cannon Ltd is an engineering company that undertakes a variety of customised jobs for a range of clients. Currently, the company is operating with significant spare capacity and has been approached by a client to perform a customised job, for which the customer is willing to pay £80,000. Cannon normally operates an absorption costing system when pricing jobs and the management accountant has collected the following information concerning the cost of the proposed job:

	£
Direct materials	40,000
Direct labour	30,000
Overheads:	
Power to operate machinery	2,000
Consumable materials (lubricants, etc.)	1,500
Depreciation on equipment	3,500
Share of fixed costs	5,000
Total cost	82,000

Required

Advise Cannon Ltd whether it should undertake this particular job.

Suggested answer

The relevant costs for this decision are the direct costs (materials and labour) and any variable overheads. It seems likely that electric power used to operate machinery, together with any consumable materials like oil, will be variable costs. These are the only additional costs that would be incurred as a result of the decision to accept the job. The company has significant spare capacity, so the fixed costs are unlikely to change as a result of undertaking this particular job. The relevant costs are, therefore:

	£
Direct materials	40,000
Direct labour	30,000
Overheads:	
Power to operate machinery	2,000
Consumable materials (lubricants, etc.)	1,500
	73,500
Price to customer	80,000
Net gain from accepting order	6,500

In the current circumstances, therefore, Cannon Ltd should accept this order.

References

Drury, C. (2008) *Management and Cost Accounting* (7th edn), London, South-Western, Cengage Learning.

Horngren, C.T., Bhimani, A., Foster, G. and Datar, S.M. (1999) *Management and Cost Accounting*, London, Prentice Hall Europe.

Lucas, M. (1999) 'The pricing decision: economists versus accountants', *Management Accounting*, vol. 77, no. 6, pp. 34–5.

Seal, W., Garrison, R.H. and Noreen, E.W. (2006) *Management Accounting* (2nd edn), Maidenhead, UK, McGraw-Hill Education.

Acknowledgements

Grateful acknowledgement is made to the following sources.

Cover image: iStockphoto.com

Illustrations

Page 20: Fortune Teller © Mike Baldwin, www.cartoonstock.com

Page 23: Re-Tooling Costs © John Morris, www.cartoonstock.com

Page 30: Grocery store © Chris Wildt, www.cartoonstock.com

Page 59: To cut down heating © Ron Morgan, www.cartoonstock.com

Every effort has been made to contact copyright holders. If any have been inadvertently overlooked the publishers will be pleased to make the necessary arrangements at the first opportunity.